The Youth Of Pakistan
Calling & Cure of Pakistan

By
Hafiza Noor-ul-Ain

BEYOND
SANITY
PUBLISHING

Beyond Sanity Publishing

Published By:
Beyond Sanity Publishing
Islamabad, Pakistan

www.beyondsanitypublishing.com

Cover Design By: Khurram Shahbaz
Edition: 1st Edition
Copies: 500 Copies
Book Layout: Team Beyond Sanity Publishing
Publisher: Beyond Sanity Publishing
Bound and Printed in Islamabad, Pakistan

ISBN 10: 1518603351
ISBN 13: 978-1518603358

Dedication

Dedicated to my Mother, who, I know,
Will always be there for me, and to the youth of my country,
For whom this book is written.

Author's Note

Our beloved homeland Pakistan is standing at this instant at one of the most sensitive points of its history when there is the darkness of hopelessness and destruction everywhere. Deaths and mostly unpredictable deaths have become a day-to-day matter for us as dozens die at the hands of terrorism every week. This havoc is tightening its siege upon us with every passing moment and so this time is the biggest test for all our abilities, patience and endurance. We are capable of protecting our own home and now we have to show it to all! We are the most zealous youth who are totally unpredictable and this would soon be revealed Insha'Allah

Everyone from us has the responsibility to put his or her part in our own betterment and hence this book could be understood as a meager attempt by an ordinary girl to make her fellow young brothers and sisters realize their capabilities and the need for their concern.

Regards,

The Author.

Contents

Chapter 1- Who Are We?

Such an open question set like this absolutely seems silly to be answered by busy people like us. We do not even have enough time to ponder upon our deeds and their outcomes so thinking about identity and purpose of existence seems foolishly meaningless. But this excuse never makes this behavior the right way to tackle things. This question set over here is, in reality, the essence of all the research and scientific development acquired so far by us human beings.

"Who am I?" is the first question that ever clicks the mind of a sensible young human being as the need to know the purpose of one's existence. One can be then provided by all essential rudiments for logical reasoning from the history of one's ancestors to sort out the question. On an individual level, everyone is equally interested in finding an answer to this and so are you and me. Every person has a specific individuality which is distinctive from everyone else. This difference in choice and thoughts defines the variations in life purposes and aims of people. But here, we are asking ourselves the question *"who are we?"* which definitely demands a more 'plural' approach. So let us discuss its possible solution on our national level.

First and most basic of all, we are human beings. More specifically, we are the proud followers of the last "Prophet of Allah" (PBUH) and then, it is us who are the most ambitious youth of an extraordinarily distinct nation....

However, we do face an apparent lack of some basic characteristics of 'normal' human beings which, at times, even brings our claim of being humans nearly at stake. The first one of these qualities is the tendency to change ourselves in order to progress. Mind you, but this change never refers to the modification of the ways of living or the copying of other nations' cultures under the name *of 'liberal enlightenment'*. Rather, this change means a positive variation in our behavior, a change in the national 'system' which is, by now, full of defects and flaws. Now let us discuss it in a more practical detail. We obviously acknowledge the well-known fact that:

"Progress needs change."

But can we apply it to our daily lives? Although, we do 'change' our fashion trends almost the fastest in the world but still or progress rate seems to be the slowest in the world. Can you tell why this is so? Obviously, it is so because we do not change ourselves in the right perspective. We do nothing except shutting our eyes and staying indoors just to save ourselves from the havoc outside in our own motherland. But we do have to come out from this darkness of obscurity and lethargy. We have to make our purpose clear first and then show others the direction to proceed. In my thinking, the system does not change because we do not change and we do not change because the system never lets us do so. But with that stupid logic, should we become like the generation which came before us and those which came earlier on in the near past? No! .... Allah has not sent us merely to eat, drink and die. If He has made us more politically and socially aware as compared to the earlier ones and has given us a greater advancement of knowledge and information technology so it means that we have a greater purpose of life as well. This is the change which is needed crucially. We should never surrender and adapt to the system but we should make the system adapt to the changes we make in it. Even when it seems nearly impossible to actually bring about a change that massive but everything has a starting point and we are going to have to create one for us.

That was what we can do about the change. Now let us discuss the second factor which is the lack of self-confidence leading to an absence of hope. This is a common practice in our society that whenever anyone steps forward to make something better for the country, mocks and scoffs are hurled from all directions including the friends and family circle. But should our ambitions be so weak to be easily dwindled by this mischief? And if they are, so we have to make them stronger. Everyone has to come forth with his or her contribution believing that there are hundreds and thousands of others who are even more patriotic and zealous about Pakistan but never got a chance to show it practically and these people would then surely back the courageous initiator. Hope in the form of positive outcomes would then automatically follow this belief and confidence.

Thirdly and most tragically, we are becoming more and more insensate with each passing day. However, although this owes more to the surrounding circumstances rather than our own lack of concern but still we do have to blame ourselves as well. Is it not true that hundreds of our Pakistani brothers, people just like us, die an unpredictable death every month and we just do nothing except watching what happened and then switching to some other channel for our 'mind relaxation' after listening to such tragic news? It never means that we don't care but the frequent repetition and continuation of these tragedies has hardened our hearts to such an extent that we hardly feel any pain for our Pakistani brothers; Muslim or not. But us having the ability of turning around the conventional rivers is also, without any doubt, a reality. What we need by now is merely a realization...

Now let us come to our identity being Muslims. We do claim to believe in the Almighty Being of Allah without any doubt. We also wear charms of His Name and cry only for Him whenever we are stuck and need help. Moreover, above all, we are *'borne Muslims'*. But is that enough? Do we act like Muslims? How many of us pray five times a day? Although paying Zakat is not yet the responsibility of most of us but what about refraining from falsehood, deceit, intermixing of truth and lies, back biting and all kinds of social abuses? However, most of you would be having the rightful justification of blaming your elders, parents and society for not teaching you the basic etiquettes and requirements for being Muslims but do you still require their concern for your path of conduct? We must be sensible enough ourselves to judge and then identify which path to follow with logical reasons. This is rightfully the time to show our maturity in the form of belief in the Day of Resurrection. We have to start our very own quest of finding what being a Muslim actually means. A huge change, perhaps a revolution is needed to make us true Muslims. The primary step of this change is the creation of a true sincere will and the help of Almighty Allah would then follow this sincerity.

Furthermore, Islam has become more to us like a ritualistic inheritance rather than a path of conduct. We, being Pakistani Muslims, are ahead of the whole Islamic world in carrying out religious rituals most enthusiastically but the main purpose of behavior betterment and lessons of brotherhood are sadly, nowhere to be seen. But we have to show the previous generations that we are never going to surrender like them. They surely did nothing other than absorbing in the already worn out 'system' and further increasing its flaws. But we have to be more truthful, sincere, patriotic and straightforward as compared to them. Our search for the right path starts from and ends as well at the one and only Holy Quran as reading its translation can reveal the answers to all our queries and can solve every problem we encounter. This is the time for us to understand our purpose of life and real status as human beings as the Holy Quran says:

"O people! Worship your Sustainer (Rabb) who created you and those who came before you so that you may learn self-restraint."(Al-Baqarah, Ayah: 21)

It also says:

"And we have not created the jinn and the mankind except for the purpose that they should worship."(Al-Zariat, Ayah: 56)

And so, friends, right there we are told in the clearest way possible that the purpose of creation is worshipping and being a slave of the Creator. How many of us even accomplish that purpose of life?

However, on our identity as Muslims, this world has forcefully put a stamp of being terrorists as well. But are we terrorists? We normally answer to this question in the simple negative as we are Muslims but not extremists or terrorists. But oppressively though, the whole world calls us so! Moreover, the Islamic countries seem unhappy at our 'most allied' alliance with the west, particularly the USA while all the western countries openly call us a terrorist nation. As the youth of this country, we are going to be the ones to whom the steering wheel of this country would be soon handed over and hence, it is our responsibility to tackle with the terrorism problem. Sadly, the meaning of the term terrorism has always been misused by our enemies and totally misunderstood by us. This is just because of the American influence on our thoughts. So when the US calls a person a national hero the whole Pakistani nation admires him and when they start calling the same person a terrorist after some time, our nation responds by doing the same. This is exactly what was done to Usama bin Ladin. After 1985, it was Usama who resisted and saved his homeland from Russian invasion and we were there at the top of the list in supporting the Taliban backed up by the USA. Then a time came when the USA itself caught an eye upon Afghanistan and all of a sudden, the whole strategy was reversed. This is not supposed to imply that Usama was a good man but what I mean to say is that our opinions should be based upon what we believe and observe, not what someone like the USA tells us.

And then the same Taliban once called Mujahideen or the 'Holy Fighters' in Afghanistan were now extremists later on to be called terrorists forcing us without any reason into the so called 'War on Terror'; all because of a terrorist attack on the US itself. It surely was a severe tragedy for the whole mankind and by all means it had to be avenged but then, every life should be equally respected, whether its an innocent Muslim dying in Palestine or an innocent Christian dying in America.

Over here, all the havoc then purely happened due to us blindly following the US agenda for 'dollars'. Then to make it worse, trained people from different nationalities, who were never Muslims but had an obvious common objective of enmity against Islam and Pakistan were poured into Afghanistan. Their get ups and language had been transformed so cunningly into the ones of local Afghani or Pakhtun people that at that time, no one really understood what had happened. The truth was unfolded when after the operations in Northern Pakistan the corpses of terrorist masterminds revealed that they weren't Muslims. The worst part is that the young boys who were given the task of exploding themselves and killing Muslims in the name of Islam were all Pakistanis of the Northern Areas. Hence, the real people who were the masterminds of all the terrorism machinery operating till now in our county were never the real Afghan Taliban . A local organisation of a broken country can never be capable of the high tech facilities and the endless supply of arms that the TTP happen to have. Hence, what happened was, and is still happening; is that funds from countries in the whole world who were interested in spoiling Pakistan- primarily the US and India- were poured into Afghanistan and then these people entered the tribal and northern areas of Pakistan to brainwash the youth there.

Surprisingly, Islam was their main weapon and the victim was also Islam. How was this havoc ever a Jihad when it was fought against fellow Muslims? From where in the Quran, Hadis or Sunnah do we learn that killing fellow Muslims is not only lawful but it even is a means of gaining Paradise? Rather, the Quran happens to have an altogether opposite perspective over this:

"And whoever kills a believer intentionally, his recompense is Hell to abide therein, and the Wrath and the Curse of Allah are upon him, and a great punishment is prepared for him." (An-Nisa, Ayah: 93)

If it is a Jihad so why is it not fought against America, India or Israel who are responsible for flowing hell of a lot of innocent Muslim blood everywhere in the world? Tragically, even after spoiling our army, destroying our economy and sacrificing millions of lives of civilians as well as soldiers for the war on terror, we could still not prove our innocence to the world and became, in the eyes of the world, the murderer as well as the one who is being murdered. Now it is obviously on us how we prove the clear but deliberately obscured difference between Pakistani Muslims and the real terrorists.

Then it is our discriminating identity for being the youth of Pakistan. We are distinctive for being the citizens of the only country created after such a massive struggle on religious or more generally, an ideological basis. Our country is the only one founded purely for Islam and for Muslims. The same fact that the name of Allah Almighty was taken in the struggle for Pakistan is the reason for a second fact that we happen to be the only nation to manage to survive the greatest hardships of all times and types. Furthermore, we are also the first and, until now, the only internationally recognized Islamic nuclear power the world has ever seen.

However, being the Pakistani youth attaches two more dignities to us. Firstly, we are the youth by which even the noble Quaid was inspired. He knew that the youth was the real power for his Pakistan Movement and also for his Pakistan. He was aware that it was the Muslim youth which could make his Pakistan Movement irresistible and it truly did. At that time, the Muslim college and university students were the main stronghold for the whole Indian Muslim community and were also the backbone of the struggle for Pakistan. This youth led by the rocky determination of Quaid made the British and the Hindus kneel in front of their desire for a separate homeland. Quaid had seen the power of the youth but his keen foresight had also seen the qualities of the 'Pakistani' youth and he fully acknowledged our capabilities and responsibilities because it was us to whom he said:

"Pakistan is proud of her youth, particularly the students who have always been in the forefront in the hour of trial and need. You are the nation's leaders of tomorrow and you must fully equip yourself by discipline, education training for the arduous task lying ahead of you. You should realize the magnitude of your responsibility and be ready to bear it."(Quaid addressing the Punjabi Muslim Students Federation at Lahore on October 31, 1947)

Quaid-e-Azam Muhammad Ali Jinnah said this as well to the youth of Pakistan:

"My young friends, I look forward to you as the real makers of Pakistan, do not be exploited and do not be misled. Create amongst yourselves complete unity and solidarity. Set an example of what youth can do."

جوال مرد کی ضربتِ غازیانہ ہوائے بیاباں سے ہوتی ہے کاری

Secondly, we are the *'Shaheens'* of the Poet of the East, Dr. Allama Muhammad Iqbal. It obviously has to be us whom he admires and addresses in his poetry as the Muslim youth. So as young Pakistanis, this should be our primary responsibility to embed in ourselves all the qualities of the true *'Shaheen'* as described by our national poet. Iqbal's poetry is easily comprehendible but extremely meaningful. The need for us is, therefore, only to understand it and then try our best to accomplish the task of becoming a *'Shaheen'* in its true verdicts. Here is a piece of Iqbal's work to make you learn what should be our goal being the *'Shaheen'* and more primarily, being the Pakistani youth:

کیا میں نے اُس خاک داں سے کنارا جہاں رزق کا نام ہے آب و دانہ

بیاباں کی خلوت خوش آتی ہے مجھ کو ازل سے ہے فطرت مری راہبانہ

نہ باد بہاری نہ گلچیں نہ بلبل نہ بیماری نغمہ عاشقانہ

خیابانیوں سے ہے پرہیز لازم ادائیں ہیں ان کی بہت دلبرانہ

یہ جھپٹنا، پلٹنا، پلٹ کر جھپٹنا   لہو گرم رکھنے کا ہے اک بہانہ

حمام و کبوتر کا بھوکا نہیں میں   کہ ہے زندگی باز کی زاہدانہ

پرندوں کی دنیا کا درویش ہوں میں
کہ شاہیں بناتا نہیں آشیانہ

Translation

I have turned away from that place in earth

Where sustenance takes the form of grain and water;

The solitude of the wildness pleases me___

By nature, I was always a hermit___;

No spring breeze, no one plucking roses, no nightingale

And no sickness of the songs of love;

One must shun the garden-dwellers___

They have much seductive charms;

The wind of the desert is what gives

The stroke of the brave youth fighting in battle its effect;

I am not hungry for pigeon or dove

For renunciation is the mark of an eagle's life;

To swoop, withdraw and swoop again

Is only a pretext to keep up the heat of the blood;

East and west_ these belong to the world of pheasants

The blue sky_ vast and boundless_ is mine!

I am the dervish of the kingdom of birds

The eagle does not make nests.)

But the purpose here is not a mere glance. I, hence, request you to fully absorb the lessons of self-respect, honor, pride, distinctiveness, remarkable aims, forbearance and patience covered so magnificently by these words.

There are many other extraordinary qualities as well which would be discussed later on as you read this book. But at this stage, I would only want you to understand who we really are, at what point we are currently standing and what status we actually deserve.

Chapter 2. Identity Matters

World War 2 had been a tragedy for Japan. The havoc which Japan faced after this four year long war is little to be seen with any other country in the history of mankind. The confidence gained by the victory in World War 1 had paved the way for Japan to attack the US controlled Pearl Harbor on 7 December, 1941 and to declare war. This attack was only done with the intentions of extending the Japanese territory and removing USA from its trade routes but this attack brought was the World War 2. Japan got initial success but when the Allies (led by the US) rose in renaissance, Japan had nothing but utter defeat and massive destruction. The atomic bombing of Hiroshima and Nagasaki on 6th and 9th of August, 1945 had led to an unconditional surrender by Japan on August 15, 1945.

Figure 5: The destruction of Japan in WWII

Its major towns were now heaps of debris, industries flattened to ground, air force completely eradicated, naval force nearly finished and land forces fully powerless. Moreover, the economy had been devastated summed up with the loss of millions of lives of armed forces and civilians and many more were also punished after the war by the Allies as war criminals....

But one can hardly believe all these facts when one comes to know the position of Japan now_ merely 67 years after that deadly war ended. According to Wikipedia; Japan, being a major economic power, has the World's third largest economy by nominal GDP and fourth largest economy by purchasing power parity. Japan is the fourth largest importer and exporter. Its Tokyo Stock Exchange is Asia's largest stock exchange.

Figure 6: The Tokyo Stock Exchange

It has a powerful industry that manufactures machinery, motor vehicles, electronics, processed food items, textile and chemical substances. It is also an influential member of the UN since 1956 and is a non-permanent member of the Security Council but is among the G4 nations seeking permanent membership. Japan has the lowest homicide rate after Singapore, greatest life expectancy and lowest infant mortality rate. As with military, although Japan has no right to declare war but it does possess nuclear power and a modernly equipped army used in international disputes and peace-keeping missions.

After reading this unbelievable contrast, most of you would be moved to think about the reasons for this incredible progress. Let us have a look at the possible situations. But wait! ..... Keep in mind that Japan had no military supremacy on whose basis it could proceed, no industries to readily provide it with resources once again, no economy to strengthen it, no favorable foreign relations which could be expected to bring in international aid and with that, it had even lost millions of working hands and many beautiful cities. So what was left there which brought them to the skies of progress and greatness once again? If we ponder upon all the circumstances again we come to know that it was actually the department of education which they had protected from the ravages of war. But through education, they had cleverly preserved the real treasure, the respect for their identity.

It was the identity which mattered!

But I have not told you this remarkable example just for fun. Apply it to your own nation. After the war ended, the Japanese did all they could to uphold their identity through their education. They taught their children to feel proud of their identity in the true sense. But can we claim that we respect our identity too? Are we sure that we are proud Pakistanis? .... In the previous chapter I explained our identity to you. Now let us discuss the importance we give to it and what importance it actually deserves.

The first part is obviously, our religion. How much honor can we claim to be having for Islam? Sadly, this 'honor' cannot even reach the limit of being able to provoke a curiosity in our minds about what Islam actually demands from us. We do 'honor' our religion by performing some rituals and these are, without any doubt, an important and extremely meritorious part of Islam. But the true spirit is more important and more meritorious but its application is always neglected. We have to learn to regard our religion as our true code of life because without becoming true proud Muslims we can just never become successful Pakistanis! We have to learn to respect it fully with all our hearts and the deepest feelings.

Then there are the language and culture which we have. Do we regard our national language as our 'national language'? I never blame you for reading, writing or speaking in English because it is the means of communication with the outer world. No doubt, our Quaid also spoke English. Learning or using English is not what matters here. What matters is the respect given to English in contrast with our national language Urdu. The real alarming situation is not the opening of English medium schools. Rather, it is that English has become a strange source of pride and people who can only speak Urdu or native languages are regarded as second or third class citizens. Not surprisingly, we are one of the very few nations who undermine their own language themselves. Do speak English whereever you are required to do so but never feel ashamed of speaking Urdu or any of your native regional mother tongues.

Secondly, how we respect our culture is also a well-known fact. We have, without any doubt, sought and gained independence from the British but our slavery to their language and culture still flourishes! We blindly follow the Western culture in order to look modern but this 'modernization' is never the key to progress. Indeed, this unconditional obedience is leading us to the same well of doom where the western societies have already fallen and are now stuck there. But even this gradual and eventual downfall of the western civilization is unable to teach us what 'modernization' actually is. With all their morals, etiquettes, family inter-relationships and social values completely eradicated, the people there are leading their lives far below the status bestowed upon human beings as the 'crown of creations'.

Last but never the least is the status we give to our identity as being Pakistanis. Any idea for the respect of this identity is smashed instantly into pieces by strange young Pakistanis when they say:

"My greatest aim of life is to find a trustworthy job abroad and to settle there with my family. Only a fool would like to stay in a country like this after completing his education. No one gives us facilities here so why should we spoil our future? And nevertheless,

WHAT HAS PAKISTAN ACTUALLY GIVEN TO US?"

Whenever I personally encounter such statement I want to cry out and tell these people what Pakistan has given us. The greatest gift which Pakistan gives us is this identity, this badge of belonging to a superb nation. Pakistan gave us independence to practice our lives freely in an Islamic way or any way we want. It is Pakistan who has saved us from the deadliness of the Hindus. If it were not for Pakistan, we would have all been lifelong slaves of brutal Hindus for generations, or nearly non-existent, or even worse. Pakistan is our home and gives us everything a home can ever promise to give. The feeling of possession that only Pakistan provides us can never be found anywhere else.

We know that one can never find solace in seeking refuge in someone else's owned territory. That is why, the real feeling of patriotism is realized only when these people actually leave Pakistan intending never to return to these dusty roads and smoky skies. They travel abroad and some of them even find and honorable place in other societies but when the laws of those 'dream' countries restrict them from practicing their religion freely, when they are rebuked as third class citizens, when they are called as the ones belonging to a terrorist nation, when they find no hospitality in return for their enthusiasm, when pangs of homesickness makes lives difficult, when not even a single familiar face is there to share joys and sorrows and when the tranquility of heart and soul is lost forever, then it dawns on them. The importance of the 'dear motherland' is only realized after passing through this phase and then the only purpose of these people's lives becomes to somehow return to the same dusty roads and smoky skies. The lyrics of the song of the Pakistani singer Nadeem Abbas so beautifully describe the story of such a person:

(Translation:

Dear country mates! I have wandered through the land,

Somewhere I cried while I somewhere smiled over the humanity,

I longed for flowers, but I have brought wounds.

Each of my wounds says

Make your country mates understand;

That we have nothing beyond the Pakistani borders,

That we have nothing beyond the Pakistani borders.)

But this argument never means that we should not even step out of the borders of Pakistan for vital purposes like education and business tours. The meaning intended here is merely that setting any other country as the final destination is a grave mistake and its consequences are the same as described above.

Another aspect of leaving Pakistan constitutes the 'brain drain'. When young graduates, doctors and other professionals leave Pakistan, they use all of the talent and education gained from the land of Pakistan for the betterment of some other country without ever realizing the severity of their need in their own motherland. The logic these talented people put forth is that when the ruling elite and governmental authorities have no regard for their talent so why should they spoil their lives? But are they the governmental authorities whom we ought to care for? No! we must stay here because we know that our country and our people need us! They need everything we have, our talent, commitment, abilities and sincerity. The only thing needed is a mindful response to these 'wailing' sounds. They do need us!

Anyhow, some young people also leave Pakistan being 'afraid' of the hopelessness and the difficulties which our country encounters. This is, by all means, the most idiotic excuse for leaving one's home saying that it is set on fire! Being Pakistanis, and above all, being Muslims, we can never be cowards to run away from problems. If problems are a reality, we have to face them and win over them in the true spirit of being Pakistani Muslims and I know we are brave enough to do so.

This detailed explanation would have made you clear of the difference between the regard we pay to our identity and the one which Japanese have. But, nevertheless, we still have time to correct ourselves and save our nation from doom. We can still do it! All we have to do is just to acknowledge the fact that in the spirit of being true Pakistanis, the sole purposes of our lives should be firstly to make ourselves feel proud of our identity and then make the world look up at our identity with envious eyes! For it is surely the only way for us to progress just as Japan did!

Chapter 3. The Best Nation?

I've been trying hard in the last chapter to convince you about the need for a nation to feel proud of its identity as it plays a key role in the progress of that particular nation. However, this is not at all the only reason for us to feel proud of our identity. We do possess a fabulous identity... but most of us do say:

"Should we feel proud of being the world's most suppressed nation being Muslims or should we feel proud for being the nation in the worst Economical and political situation as Pakistanis?"

I would try my best to answer this objection in this chapter.

Our identity as Muslims would be the first topic of discussion. One single ayah of the Holy Quran eliminates all confusion in this area by saying:

"You are the best nation brought forth for the guidance of mankind..."
(Al-e-Imran, Ayah: 110)

This is a true reason enough for pride but curious minds search for more. So let me tell you just that. The greatest discriminative gift awarded to us as Muslims is the unparalleled code of life. Today as well, not a single religion of the whole world is capable enough to compete with Islam in the perfect alignment, compatibility, practicality and rationalism its prescribed code of life contains. This code of life has been bestowed upon us in the form of the ultimately Divine Holy Quran and the all Praiseworthy Sunnah of the Holy Prophet (PBUH). The Holy Quran being the last and complete Divine Book has opened up all gates of enlightenment and Divine guidance for the whole mankind. Distinctions are many. Firstly, it is the only book of the world whose contents can never be changed. The earlier books of Jews and Christians, the 'Ahl-e-kitaab', are not present today in their true form. Being revealed originally in Hebrew language, today not a single copy of Bible or other books exists in Hebrew. Rather, they consist of versions with neither any solid proof of authenticity nor any linkage to the times when the original ones came. However, the Holy Quran is read everywhere in Arabic, the same language in which it was revealed. There are millions in this world who know Arabic and there are also millions of Muslims who know each and every word of the Holy Quran by heart. Moreover, one of the seven authentic copies of the '*Mushaf*' compiled by Hazrat Abu Bakr (RA) still exists today.

Figure 7: The oldest copy of Holy Quran, from the era of Hazrat Usman (RA)

But these are only the worldly reasons which never allow even any minute error to creep in the text of the Holy Quran but indeed it is Allah who is fulfilling His promise:

"Surely We have revealed the Book of Remembrance and We shall preserve it."(Al-Hijr, Ayah: 90)

Furthermore, all the social, moral, religious, economical, financial, political, academic, individual as well as national laws have been stated and described so clearly in the Holy Quran that anyone from any field of life can find answers and guidance in it. Another beautiful aspect is the appealing mode of communication adopted in the Holy Quran. It is its magic that if one listens to its recitation in a melodious voice, even in Arabic which is not understandable to most of us, one is so enchanted by the words that one can never restrict oneself from pausing and listening to it carefully. If we read its translation, it is so comprehensive and mind catching that it can never be believed to be anything other than being the Holy Revelation of Allah Almighty the Creator of the universe. The logics in this unique book are so rational that no counter-logic can ever be produced by any human authority against it. These superiorities of this book over the books of the rest of the world are surely a symbol of pride for us along with being a place to find solace and tranquility of soul.

Then comes the practical demonstration of this code of life in the form of the Sunnah of the Holy Prophet (PBUH). Humanity cannot give even a single example for matching him in any aspect of his perfect demonstration of the highest limits of behavior greatness, patience, truthfulness, honesty, forgiveness, forbearance, promise-keeping and each and every aura of human personality. He spent his whole life in extreme hardships and suffered lot but he never turned back; never gave up and he did this only for us and for our betterment in the Hereafter. Above all, he was the last Messenger of Allah and an honor for humanity.

Figure 8: Our Beloved Prophet (PBUH)

The Holy Quran says about him:

"And you (stand) on an exalted standard of character."(Al-Qalam, Ayah: 4)

So shouldn't we feel proud to be the members of the Ummah of such a great Prophet (PBUH)? Of course we should! However, here I would like to clarify that this explanation never tells you that feeling proud for Quran and Sunnah is your destiny. Rather, it means that this pride and sense of dignity is only the first step towards us becoming practical Muslims in the true meanings.

There are lots of other things as well which only we possess with no other nation resembling us. We Muslims, as a nation are without question the pioneers for true and humble leadership, democracy, defined and implemented human rights, legal system, a law enforcement police force, just taxation rules, independent judiciary, unmatched religious tolerance, uniformity of law for every citizen, rights for women in every field, elimination of any cast, color, creed or race discrimination, warfare rules, defined social and moral codes and hence, we are the originators of true civilization. The golden period of the era of Holy Prophet (PBUH) and the Rightly Guided Caliphs is an extraordinary period of the best government the whole mankind had ever seen before. This is, obviously, another pride for us being Muslims.

Then comes the role played by our admirable ancestors in the field of education and science. For Chemistry, its origin owes to Jabir bin Hayyan who invented nitric and sulfuric acid and discovered methods of refining. In Mathematics, Al-Khwarizmi had no match as he invented Algebra and also extended a considerable work on equations. Al-Razi and Al-Zahrawi were incredible in medicine with Al-Zahrawi as the inventor of nearly all modern surgical methods along with their equipment while Al-Razi discovered small pox and measles. Muslim Physicians and astronomy specialists were many including Al-Kindi, the Banu Musa brothers and Omar Khayam. These physicians originated automation, calculated the length of the year, found out the diameter of the earth and also formulated the first calendar of the world. Then it is travel with our Ibn-e-Batuta as the first person to have travelled so extensively around the world. The libraries and madrassahs of Qartabah and Al-Hamrah were the centers of worldwide education and were located in the glorious Muslim Spain.

Figure 9: (from left to right) Jabir bin Hayyan, Al-Khwarizmi, Al-Razi, Al-Zahrawi, Al-Kindi, Ibn-e-Batuta

Those who claim so arrogantly today for being the sole masters of science and technology were experiencing their dark age at that time. Book reading or even book keeping was a sin in Europe with no other penalty except death. There was not a single civilization flourishing there at that time and when the wealthiest of these wild nomads could scarcely see gold, Muslims even had the armors of their horses layered with gold. Even today, all their fame in science and technology is bound to rely completely on the extensive books written by Muslim medieval scientists.

Moreover, another source of honor is our valor, the official trademark for Muslim armies. They were our forefathers who ruled the whole world for centuries and it was not only the rule which they did. Instead, they also taught the whole world the manners to lead life. How was an almost weaponless army of 313 under Prophet Muhammad (PBUH) able to defeat a dozens-of-times-better-equipped Quraish army of 1000 at Badr? How was an army of 3000 under Hazrat Khalid bin Waleed (RA) able to defeat a 100,000 army of Roman Christians at Mautta? How was Hazrat Ali (RA) able to defeat the Jews of Khyber so easily with a much smaller army? How our Prophet (PBUH) captured Makkah so peacefully and forgave everyone from his worst enemies? How was Sultan Salahuddin made capable of re-capturing Jerusalem and how, instead of taking revenge of hundreds of thousands of Muslims slaughtered 90 years back in the same city, he actually forgave the whole Christian community and transferred them safely to their Christian castles? The answer lies in the fact that they never fought for triumphs or for lands. Rather, the reason for fighting was the desire for martyrdom as no one can defeat an army of men when each and every one of them are totally fearless of death. On worldly level, they fought for the freedom of humanity from barbarian rules as Muslim armies freed nations whenever their rulers were being unjust to them; hence setting a beautiful example for mankind to follow. This made them an irresistible force and the desire for martyrdom is what we still own as a sign of our self-confidence and pride.

Figure 10:
Wars against the crusaders led by Sultan
Salahuddin Ayyubi were one of the best examples
of Muslim valor and greatness

Iqbal had said:

رِٹا یا قیصــرو کسری کے استبداد کو جس نے
وہ کیا تھا، زورِحیدرؓ، فقرِ بُوذرؓ، صدقِ سلمانیؓ

(Translation:

What was it that erased the tyranny of Caesar and Cyrus?

The power of Hyder (RA), the asceticism of Bu Dharr (RA), the truth of
Salman (RA).)

This was a pretty detailed description for us being the best nation on religious basis. Now I would come on to the topic for us being the best nation on country basis. This surely seems to be a dream statement for most of us but believe me! Nature has actually made us to be the best nation. However, the need is just to realize this fact, be confident, and feel proud as the first step to our national betterment.

What to say of natural resources or our national potential, I would just start with the scratch; the location of Pakistan. Strategically, Pakistan is located in the middle of South Asia giving it a huge strategic benefit. Firstly, the Karachi Port is in the central position for trading with the Middle East and the West as well. It is a natural warm water harbor and can act as a refueling stop for ships due to this central position. The Gwadar Port lies so close to the 'Strait of Hormuz' (official routes for ships carrying cargo from Gulf States) that it can easily earn a huge foreign exchange for Pakistan. The neighboring countries like Afghanistan and China have no access to the sea so it can easily serve as a route for them bringing taxes to Pakistan. Almighty has given the Jinnah Terminal of Karachi Airport such a central position that many of air routes connecting the East and the West pass through it. This can also be immensely beneficial, but this natural favor upon Karachi is being constantly used up by the Dubai International Airport.

Figure: 11: Gwardar Port

Figure 12: Jinnah Terminal, Karachi

Pakistan connects the CAS Republics and Iran to countries on its Eastern side so any gas pipeline between them would pass through Pakistan becoming an obvious source of income.

While talking about climate and terrain, Pakistan stands unmatched here as well. Pakistan is one of the few nations of the world gifted with all four regularly changing seasons. The location and topography of Pakistan brings in good rain in almost every season meeting requirements for the agriculture of the country. The abundance of rivers in the Northern and Eastern parts of Pakistan is a provider of fresh water all the yearlong with a minimal of natural floods occurring in an area so densely overtook by rivers. Then it is the awesome topography. It is a well-known fact that a country with all five kinds of landscapes including mountains, rivers, plateaus, deserts and coastline, is bound to progress. And by the Grace of Almighty, we have everything.

Figure 13: The K-2, Thar Desert,

Figure 14: River Indus, Clifton Beach (Karachi)

From the junction of three greatest ranges of snow covered peaks (Karakoram, Himalaya and Hindu Kush) to burning deserts with scorching heat of the sun, from 8610 meters above sea level (K-2 height) to coastline at sea level and from the mighty Indus river and its huge tributaries to the plateaus of Potwar and Balochistan, everything is incredibly present over here.

Now let us come to the power resources. We possess all possible sources for renewable power generation invented by mankind till now. We do have everything including the winds of southern Pakistan easily capable to activate windmills, many rivers and waterfalls to generate hydel power, waves in the Arabian sea to generate power through wave energy, numerous rivers able to generate tidal energy, junction of seismic plates to produce geothermal power and above all, we have long sunny days throughout the year for easy solar power generation. Now, if we talk about the non-renewable power resources, Pakistan has coal in lower Sindh and other areas in such abundance that if properly used, it can serve even more than the oilfields of the Gulf states.

Figure 15: The Thar coalfield, Lower Sindh

 Balochistan has a huge gold mine but this natural treasure, like most of the others, is unused up to date. The gas reserves of Sui fulfill the demand of the whole country. Moreover, a considerable amount of inorganic natural resources lie here in Pakistan.

After discussing all this, now I would come to the potential and national talent that we possess. Hundreds of Pakistanis prove themselves in the world every year by winning internationally appreciated laurels for the country. We are the nation which produces brilliants like Arfa Karim and geniuses like Dr. Abdul Qadeer Khan.

Figure 16: Dr. Abdul Qadeer Khan & Arfa Karim Randhawa

Millions of us are serving abroad with their abilities and are sending remittances to Pakistan. Our nation has always been known for its diligence. But above all, 'we' are the greatest treasure for our nation. With all our talent and skills we are the active workforce of Pakistan which has to be sincerely hardworking in its conduct and extremely patriotic in its behavior. Then there are other reasons for our pride including us being the seventh nuclear power of the whole world and the first nuclear power of the Islamic world. We are also the fourth largest cruise missile producer and should be proud to be so. In short, our wealth as the Pakistani nation is limitless in every aspect.

After believing in all these aspects, which one of you would still be able to speak of Pakistan as a poor country. No, we are naturally rich! Being potentially richer than any other nation in every aspect, we are surely the best nation being both Muslims and Pakistanis. So, I am justly proud to be so, aren't you?

Chapter 4. True Leadership

After a long journey, the Byzantine envoy had finally reached Madinah, the capital of the greatest empire of the whole world. Dressed in the finest clothes of the era and accompanied by dozens of slaves and every possible source of luxury, the envoy had tried to display the greatness of the Byzantine Empire fully. The ambassador was aware that he was about to meet the Muslim 'emperor' who had proved so undefeatable in wars. But the envoy was rather disappointed as he could not find even a single soul in the city who could welcome his arrogant entry and moreover, he had also failed to find the emperor's palace. He searched for the palace in the whole city and was finally moved to ask a resident about their 'emperor'. In reply, the man pointed towards someone and the ambassador could not help but gasp unbelievably. The 'emperor' he was expecting to find was actually sleeping under a tree using a brick as his pillow. That 'emperor' was one of the greatest leaders of all times, Amir-ul-Momineen Hazrat Umar (RA) for whom even the Western historians say:

"If there would have been one more Umar (RA) in the history of Islam, the whole world would have been Muslim."

Dear brothers and sisters, this historic account was only one of the innumerable examples set by Hazrat Umar (RA) to explain the meaning of true leadership to the whole world; and this is our topic at the moment. Till now, we have thoroughly discussed our responsibility of feeling proud of our identity, the necessity of this feeling and the reasons for our pride. Recently, we have proved that we are the best nation with both criteria concerning religion and country. But now another question rises. Why are we not the best nation in terms of the criteria set by the world even when we have everything? Neither in religion nor in countries do we 'seem' to be the best. Why is this so? I would discuss religious weakness in the next chapter but in this one, I would tell you about the very thing we unfortunately lack and hence, as the Pakistani nation, despite having everything, we are not even able to stand on our own feet or protect our own people. That thing is true leadership!

Before plunging into any further detailed comparisons of past and present, I would firstly like to give you a glance of the real prescription of true leadership.

The foremost and simplest quality of a leader is that he is at least better than the people who are led by him and most justly, only due to this reason leaders are chosen. Leaders act as a role model for the masses and hence, they must be as perfect as possible in character, behavior, education, knowledge, foresight, decision making, mode of conduct. However, in an Islamic society, another quality of a leader being the best possible Muslim amongst them also becomes binding. If the leader is the Head of the State, the limitations are narrowed further and restrictions tighten. Now, the leader is to be the most patriotic as well and has to prefer even a petty issue of the state over his everything. Here, telling you an example seems necessary. Once a man from amongst the local people of Madinah came to see Hazrat Umar (RA) and found him doing some calculations about the State Treasury in the light of a lamp. When the man approached him and told that he had to discuss some personal matter, Hazrat Umar (RA) immediately blew off the lamp and then asked him to proceed. On being asked about the reason, he stated that the oil in the lamp was from state treasury and he could not use the people's money for a matter other than state issues. This is the real concept of a leader's sense of responsibility and patriotism. Furthermore, a leader has always to be one from amongst the common people. This is essential because he can only know and understand the people's problems if he has ever lived like them. Therefor, a feudal can only be a ruler and can never be a leader. Rather ironically, our MNAs and MPAs class is almost completely a group of feudal lords!

So I have clearly jotted down the qualities a leader has to possess. Now let me come to the way he has to lead the people. As a leader is a role model so he has to make the people obey his orders by practical demonstration giving them an example rather than mere verbal dictation. A leader's coming to leadership and going from leadership should be in the hands of the people and hence, the leader enables and empowers the people. He has to be easily accessible for even the most common people and everyone from amongst his people should have the right to freely suggest a logical reason for the leader to abandon his post. And the suggestions of the people should also be valued. The leader has also to motivate people to do better and better for their own good and for the good of the state. Lastly, a true leader is always to lead with humility as he always credits the people for every milestone achieved and every step proceeded towards national progress. In short, all the qualities and limitations for a true Muslim leader can be summarized by what Hazrat Abu Bakr (RA) said in his first speech after assuming the office of Khilafat:

"I have been elected as your Ameer, although I am not better than you. Help me, if I am in the right, set me right if I am in the wrong; obey me as long as I obey Allah and His Prophet (PBUH); when I disobey Him and His Prophet (PBUH), then obey me not."

Now, sit back, pause, and ponder! Think of the status of Hazrat Abu Bakr (RA) in the early Muslim community as being the first amongst men to embrace Islam, the first amongst the people to be given the glad tidings of paradise in their lifetime ('Ashrah Mubasharah'), the companion of Holy Prophet (PBUH) during migration and the Imam of Muslims when the Holy Prophet (PBUH) was ill. Now read his speech again and just imagine the level of humility he had. Then think of the status Hazrat Umar (RA) had as the great 'Faruq' (distinguisher of truth and falsehood), the top of the consultants of Holy Prophet (PBUH), the one whose suggestion was firstly opposed by people but then was confirmed by Allah Almighty through His Revelations, the second of the Ashrah Mubasharah and one of the bravest Muslims. Now imagine his humility by reading this incident. When the Muslim army commander conquered the city of Jerusalem, the Patriarch surrendered conditionally asking that the caliph should come himself to receive the city keys. Now, Hazrat Umar (RA) was coming with a slave and they both had only a single camel on which they both rode with turns. When the Patriarch came out with his team to receive the 'caliph', the slave was riding and Hazrat Umar (RA) was walking by shunning all popular trends of garb and court and leaving the city dwellers gasping with awe. Such was their greatness and so was the greatness of their empires.

Now compare this humility with the level of humility our leaders have. Our 'leaders' (rulers) require a perfect royal-standard protocol for every step they take and feel no shame even when most of them are aware of the situation their country is facing. For what 'extraordinary' quality are they showing this haughtiness? Do they consider themselves to be better than Hazrat Abu Bakr (RA) or Hazrat Umar (RA) and that is why they display such arrogance in contrast with the mind-blowing humility shown by those true leaders? In reality, our so-called 'leaders' in the ruling elite do not possess even a single quality matching the criteria set for leadership. A lot of our people are better then them in talents, personalities, patriotism and above all, religion. The way they are 'leading' us is also no secret to the world. One must wonder about the fact that even when we have so much potential why do we need so much foreign aid and when we get that aid, why are we not able to actually see the money being used on our country? The answer is the exploitation of the potential which is non-existent, all thanks to our leaders.

They are, by no means, worthy of ruling such a country and have no right to devastate our country's treasures. So my friends! This is how only a lack of a sincere leadership can lead the best nation to destruction. We know that we naturally possess everything but we cannot use whatever we have for our benefit just because of the rulers.

And just look at our generosity_ we have put the thieves ourselves into the treasury and now we cry for inflation, energy crisis, unemployment, terrorism and a hell of a lot of problems which are inevitable under such a 'leadership'.

Let me explain it to you with an example. Just take our national talent for instance, for which our Quaid said:

"It is in your hands, we undoubtedly have talents. Pakistan is blessed with enormous resources and potential. Providence has endowed us with all the wealth of nature and now it lies on man to make the best of it."

But today, we have a pathetic literacy rate even after such talents. Our government explains it by excusing for a lack of funds. But can a sensible man ever believe this lie when we know that our 'leaders' do beg for so much foreign aid and they also implement so many taxes on us? Then, we also know that trillions are spent monthly on the luxuries and tax non-payments of these 'leaders' even when not to mention the trillions they looted and are still robbing from our motherland. They are ruining our talents and are so actively, and unfortunately, successfully transforming a diligent, talented and patriotic youth into a mere bunch of uncivilized street-wanderers. Their sins are unforgivable and there conduct utterly shameless!

Another important link to these 'leaders' are the feudal people bringing in the feudalism problem. But this feudalism prospers because of corrupt leadership and the corrupt leadership is attained by feudalism. These feudal lords then influence the judiciary, police and legal system cunningly eliminating justice from the society with such expertise that common people like us do not even understand what is happening. The feudal lords mainly of the rural areas of Punjab and Sindh have created little empires of their own where, being uneducated themselves, they treat their subjects as their personal authority. How they manipulate the police and the locals of their area is not a stranger to any Pakistani. This is actually a spiral which is slowly but steadily leading us towards doom.

Therefore, every problem we as the Pakistani nation have today links back to a lack of true leadership and hence, all our catastrophic circumstances owe merely to this single but grave reason. The power and energy crises exist because we do not use our natural resources the way they should be used. The alarmingly low literacy rate exists because the priority of our governments over the years has simply never been education as is evident from the share the education sector is given from the budget and also from the pitiful condition of our government schools. The unemployment exists because we cannot use our natural resources to build industries and because we cannot use our own talented manpower to create; the scientific or technological innovation and research part is not even in the dictionary of our rulers. We are far behind than we deserve in all kinds of sports because the criteria there is also obviously not merit. Our police department is useless because it is corrupt which is also due to serious mis-management giving them more authority and less payment indirectly urging them to use the authority to earn money in unlawful ways. We do not have justice in our society because our political 'leaders' directly interfere with the judiciary and legal system as the law is not even applicable to our 'leaders' and their progeny. Our youth is being exploited by Western or Indian media because our society is unable to provide them with something better and productive to do. And so, the world dares to call us a failed state even when we are the best of them all only, only because we do not have a true leadership that could give the right direction to the country and its people.

However, like everything else this problem has also got a solution. We are the next generation whom these traitors in the disguise of feudal lords, rulers and corrupt 'leaders' would have to face. We are not stupid enough to be be-fooled by their cleverness, are we? I hope not. We should know that it is on our shoulders where all their strength rests and we can easily throw them into the depths of under-land whenever we want but for that we require unity. We have to realise that they are simply not worth this country and this nation. A majority of us is better than them in sincerity and patriotism so why should we accept the same feudal lords and their generations to rob us over and over again. We have got to get rid of these people and then establish a new Pakistan on the basis of what nature has bestowed upon us. After all, we have to show the world as well that we are the best nation!

Chapter 5. Our Ancestors and Us!

کبھی اے نوجوانِ مسلم! تدبر بھی کیا تونے   وہ کیا گردوں تھا تو جس کا ہے اک ٹوٹا ہوا تارا

تجھے اس قوم نے پالا ہے آغوشِ محبت میں   کچل ڈالا تھا جس نے پاؤں میں تاجِ سرِ دارا

تمدن آفریں خلاقِ آئینِ جہاں داری   وہ صحرائے عرب یعنی شترِبانوں کا گہوارا

سماں الفقرِ فخری کا رہا شانِ امارت میں   "باآبِ رنگ و خال و خط چہ حاجت روئے زیبارا"

گدائی میں بھی وہ اللہ والے تھے غیور اتنے   کہ منعم کو گدا کے ڈر سے بخشش کا نہ تھا یارا

غرض میں کیا کہوں تجھ سے کہ وہ صحرا نشیں کیا تھے   جہاں گیر و جہاں دار و جہاں بان و جہاں آرا

اگر چاہوں تو نقشہ کھینچ کر الفاظ میں رکھ دوں   مگر تیرے تخیل سے فزوں تر ہے وہ نظارا

تجھے آبا سے اپنے کوئی نسبت ہو نہیں سکتی   کہ تو گفتار وہ کردار تو ثابت وہ سیارا

گنوا دی ہم نے جو اسلاف سے میراث پائی تھی   ثریا سے زمیں پر آسماں نے ہم کو دے مارا

Translation:

O Muslim youth, have you ever stopped and pondered?

Of which sky was it, that you are now a fallen star!

You were nurtured in the loving care of such a people

Who trampled the crowns of royalty under their feet.

They established exalted civilizations, providing law (Shariat) and leadership

Those desert folk from Arabia, who cradled their camels.

The simple life was the pride they had in their deeds of glorious show

How does the lovely face feel need of rouge, and mole and art?

They lived for Allah with such modest

With such pride, that the generous dare not give them alms.

Upon impulse, what can I say to you regarding those who were those Desert folk

Except conquerors, emperors, protectors and illuminators of the world!

If I wish, I could take those visions and put them into words

Perhaps that spectacle would be far better than all of your thoughts.

You cannot claim any relationship with your Forefathers

You merely speak while they acted, you stay rooted while they went forth (like a planet).

We have de-serrated that we inherited from our Predecessors

So the Heavens exiled and pelted us, from amongst the stars down to earth.)

This poem of Dr. Allama Muhammad Iqbal most beautifully describes the difference between us and our ancestors and clearly defines the reason for our pitiful status in the world as the Muslim Ummah. In the third chapter I explained all our features which can contribute to make us the best nation as Muslims but despite all these attributes, our standings in the world are pathetic. The only reason for this is whatever has been described in the poem above, and that is, our failure to become like our ancestors. The Holy Quran, without any doubt, describes us as the best nation but it only does so with a condition. It says:

"You are the best nation brought forth for the guidance of mankind: (because) you command righteousness, forbid evil and believe in Allah."(Al-e-Imran, Ayah: 110)

Our failure to fulfill this condition stops us from being the best nation like our ancestors. We do possess the same Holy Quran as them, the same Sunnah, and obviously, the same code of life, so why are we not like them? It is our behavior to our religion which leads to this differentiation. Anyhow, in order to provide you a comparison, I would describe in detail the qualities of both.

So, let us first discuss all the attributes of our Muslim ancestors. The first and foremost quality that they owned was being a true Muslim with its deepest spirit practically implemented in their lives. They offered all obligatory services required by a Muslim but in addition, they were honest and modest as well. They accepted and acted upon Islam as a code of life and sought answers to all their queries in Holy Quran. They fulfilled all requirements of Islam and purposefully learnt and adopted every hidden lesson in all obligations. They understood the Holy Quran and transferred its verses into their practical routine life to the farthest possible extent. They were truthful in their talk and sincere in their conduct. Their behavior was a living translation of the moral values set by the Holy Quran. With an unparalleled honesty and unmatched modesty, they were utterly practical in everything they learnt from the Holy Quran, Hadis and the Sunnah. Furthermore, the grandeur of humility which they truly possessed was also incredible as is described in the poem I quoted at the start of this chapter. Their life histories reveal the fact that they had well understood the purpose of their lives according to Islam as to worship Allah (Huqooq-Ullah) and to serve His humanity (Huqooq-ul-Ibad). But the greatest quality of all, they loved Allah and His Prophet (PBUH) in its true verdicts. The Muslim nation was at its climax in those days and this pride was reflected in their lives as everyone strived and competed with others to become a better Muslim.

Secondly, they were the best human beings also who had ever evolved on the surface of the earth. They had the greatest regard for humanity as taught by Islam. They heartily respected the lives, possessions and honors of all of their fellow beings. They showed ultimate religious tolerance and hence, no religious cruelties or brutalities were to be found in their territory. They were truly the first fully civilized nation of the world which even had rules of waging war in order to maintain peace to every possible extent even when in a war. They had every modern department held firmly in its right place. So to sum up, humanity lived in peace with them and justice prevailed in the land on which those great people lived.

Thirdly, it was their bravery which boosted their enthusiasm and spurred their ambitions. They were fearless of everything except Allah and this was the reason for them ruling the world for centuries. With people like Hazrat Khalid bin Waleed (RA), the 'Sword of Allah' and Hazrat Ali bin Abi Talib (RA), the 'Lion of Allah' as the predecessors, and commanders like Tariq bin Ziyad and Muhammad bin Qasim as the successors, they were just undefeatable.

Figure 17: M. Bin Qasim

Fearlessness running in their veins and the religion of peace (Islam) implanted in their souls became the reason for them winning millions of hearts and hence, Islam spread rapidly. They feared nothing except Allah, not even death and this desire for martyrdom made them the greatest armed force of the whole world. They could defeat enemy forces even ten times larger just because of their religious zeal and then obviously, the help from Almighty paved their way to triumphs.

"If there are twenty steadfast persons amongst you, they will overcome two hundred, and if there be a hundred steadfast persons they will overcome a thousand of those who disbelieve, because they (the disbelievers) are the people who do not understand." (At-Taubah, Ayah: 65)

Then comes the regard they had for education. In those eras when in Europe, even book reading was considered a crime, Muslims upheld education as their greatest priority understanding its importance in Islam from the Holy Quran and Sunnah. They were great scholars and experts of a range of subjects covering medical science, physics, astronomy, astrology, chemistry, mathematics and of course, religious studies.

Figure 18: Muslim medieval scientists at work

This respect was the reason for the fact that all technological and scientific development stands on the foundation of the treasure of books written by our ancestors. These books were our heirloom but carelessness poured them into the enemy's hands. Now Europeans haughtily claim all development to be theirs even after knowing the fact that they would have still been in their dark ages if it was not for the research books written by Muslim scientists and stolen from Muslim Spain.

However, another significant quality they owned was the practical belief they had on the accountability of the Day of Judgement and hence, they tried to prepare as well as possible for the interview in the meeting with our Creator, Sustainer and Helper.

Now let me take you out of the imaginations of that golden era and throw reality upon you in order to awaken you. This contrast is alarming and tragic enough to make us feel extremely shameful for ourselves.

Let us first talk about us being Muslims. Islam is never changed as it is perfect enough to adjust it to every stage of human development and enlightenment. But still there is so much difference in what they considered Islam to be and what our practical beliefs about Islam are. Tragically enough, our so called 'Islamic Republic' society scoffs at anyone who tries to stick to the religion of Allah and many people even dare to call these 'normal Muslims' as being the extremist Talibans. Moreover, we are mere ritualistic people and above all, we are Muslims only because we were born in a Muslim family. We have no quality matching any criteria set in the Holy Quran for being a Muslim and even unluckily, we feel no shame for being like that. We never realize the golden and so comfortable code of life set in the Holy Quran but instead, we are following the Western nations towards the well of doom. In fact for us, it is just a book covered in 'Ghulaf' and placed somewhere high in the house as a form of respect. We never bother to even touch it except for the purpose of authenticating our oaths, blames, promises or claims. We never open it and try to study or understand it even after knowing that reading even a word of the Holy Quran is such a meritorious act that its reward is unimaginable.

Figure: 19, The Holy Quran

Only a small fraction of us claims to love Allah and His Prophet (PBUH) but still none of even this fraction can prove this claim practically. Hence, we never stand capable enough to even call us Muslims except *some* righteous fellows still persisting in a mesh of evil knotted tightly together.

Then comes our comparison with them as being humans. Humanity starts from mercy, gratitude, honor, humility and civilization. But, unfortunately we have lost everything from amongst them. We have no moral or ethic values leftover in us as we abuse each other loudly with shameful words while standing in the streets. We have a very little or no modesty even towards the members of the opposite gender and without modesty, claims of belief in Almighty have no actuality because Holy Prophet (PBUH) said:

"Faith and modesty are friends; when one is taken away, the other follows it."

Figure 20: Famous authentic collections of 'Ahadis'

Furthermore, we cheat each other, deceit and lie everyday even without recognizing the amount of hellfire we are rapidly accumulating for ourselves to be burnt in. We feel no pain for our fellow human beings and this self-centered attitude takes away any thought of the presence of sympathy or mercy in us. Humility is smashed into pieces by our self-righteous attitude which burns away any feeling of respect to the rival group and hence fights and quarrels from individual to social to provincial to governmental level follow this behavior. Civilization is nowhere to be seen as brutality, injustice, cast and creed discrimination and most importantly every kind of social abuse is not only prevailing but flourishing. We give and take bribery and consume hellfire every day. So, in my thinking, we have no quality left except our physical structure to be able to make us even 'look-like' humans. But here as well, we do have some extra-ordinary 'humans' still surviving!

Now, let us talk about the preference we give to education. We, the Pakistani youth, are in general, fed up of education if I describe it in simple words. In fact, we have even lost our grounds about the real purpose of education. Well, I never blame you! It definitely is on our parents and the society about how they tell us about education. We consider education as a means of livelihood for our upcoming life and a 'better, bright future' in this world. However, the real purpose of education that is, to make us better human beings is forsaken. But most primarily, we should educate ourselves, not for anyone or anything else, but just because our Creator and Sustainer demands us to do so. He truly said in the first revelation:

"Read! In the name of thy Lord who created. Created man out of a (mere) clot of congealed blood. Read! And thy Lord is most bountiful. He taught man the use of the pen. Taught man what he knew not."(Al-Alaq; Ayah: 1-5)

These ayahs reflect the importance of education in Islam and the purpose of education that should be present in our practical lives.

Now, this behavior of indifference towards studies has not come without a reason. So beware, our enemies are very cunning in designing plots. The first and foremost part of this conspiracy is the

Indian media which has truly exploited us. But are we fools to be morally devastated by this open conspiracy? Please say no! The ever-increasing debris shown in their movies is not designed to make their youth socially abusive_ all this is already common there. It is for us, the Pakistani youth. For sure it is designed to make us socially unacceptable for being called honorable members of a Muslim society. But can we let them win? We have all our values set by the Holy Quran and our country's rules. We have to fail them here as well and we will Insha Allah! Then comes another ravage, the 'facebook'. Our behavior towards education owes to this 'blessing' as well which is further summed up with the mobile.

Figure 21: The Facebook and cell phones are one of the greatest deviations from study today

Although, I never intend to make you completely cut off from the society. Rather, I just want to make you understand one thing. Every facility has two types of uses, positive and negative_ with the negative as always being the one which is more attractive and seductive. Now it is on our courage how we stop ourselves from tumbling to the negative side and keep ourselves firmly on the positive one.

Lastly, I would sadly talk about our current belief on accountability. I would say that we, in general, lack this as well. We do commit sins and everyone does so because no one is perfect! But the real pity is that we do not have even the slightest fear of the Day of Judgement. We forget that someone is there, seeing and hearing everything we do. How can we forget this when we claim to believe that He have us eyes? So can't the Creator of our sense of sight Himself see everyone and everything? Allah says this in the Holy Quran:

"Does he think no one sees him? Did We not give him two eyes?"(Al-Balad; Ayah: 7and 8)

Furthermore, we are unfortunately following the Western agenda of 'one life, enjoy it fully'. The Western people say:

"A day well spent is all what you have."

But our Muslim agenda says something else. It describes this world as a temporary test for the Hereafter and hence we should prepare for that because our Holy Prophet (PBUH) said:

"This world is a sowing ground for the Hereafter."

That was all about the comparison. But here, I would surely wish to make one thing crystal clear to you. The intention behind this comparison was never to make you hopeless or to tell the world about our flaws. Rather, for you it is an obvious lesson and the world it is an announcement that if our forefathers with the same blood in their veins as ours can lead the world on the basis of these principles so we can also do this. The thing needed is just to inculcate all these qualities as far as it is in our reach, in our-selves. We have mighty potential and great technological advancements. Our lives are not so spare to be squandered in trivialities. We have just to be positive and courageous in the usage of all facilities and become like our ancestors once again to reach our zenith and to fulfill our destiny as Iqbal says:

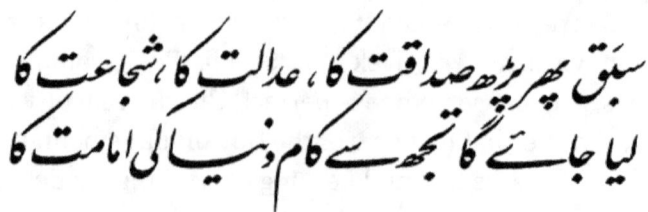

(Translation:

Read again the lesson of truth, of justice and of valor!

You will be asked to do the work of taking the responsibility of the world.)

Chapter 6. United we stand, Divided we fall

The migration to Madinah was surely a great triumph for the Prophet of Islam (PBUH). Allah had now granted Muslims a place, a state of their own where they could independently worship Him and fulfill all services of Islam in their real spirit. But migrations always bring immigrants which need to be settled and inhabited. The 'Hijrat' had brought hundreds of 'Muhajirs' (emigrants) to Madinah and their settlement was necessary. With the approval of Almighty, Holy Prophet (PBUH) gathered all emigrants and all residents of Madinah in the house of Hazrat Anas (RA). He then formulated a form of brotherhood, which is an unmatched example of unity in the human history for all times. He just took out the hand of a Muhajir and put it into one from the Ansar and the two were declared as brothers. The Ansars had then to provide initial help and settlement to their Muhajir brothers while Muhajirs intended to stand on their feet soon. The method was, of course, great but the response was even more incredible!

The Ansars took their Muhajir buothers to their houses and then history saw a selflessness never seen before. Every house of Madinah, whether big or small, was being divided into two with not even a wink of injustice. All the properties, the agricultural lands, date palms, houses and even each and every household item was divided into two parts and one was given to the Muhajir brother. They were not blood relations nor were they tribal companions. In fact, they had nothing in common except Islam. It was truly the bond of Islamic love which had overwhelmed their hearts. The Ansars could now even lay their lives if their Muhajir brothers wanted so. This was the initialization, a perfect foundation for the supreme building of Islamic inter-relationship and unity to be constructed. It was surely a gift of Almighty as is said in the Holy Quran:

"And remember with gratitude Allah's favor on you; for you were enemies and He joined your hearts in love so that by His grace you

became brothers; and you were on the brink of the pit of fire and He saved you from it. Thus Allah makes His signs clear to you, that you may be guided." (Al-e-Imran; Ayah: 103)

It was this level of unity with which the initial band of 313 holy fighters defeated 1000 infidels who were also many times superior in war equipment. Then this band grew and eventually the whole world crumpled at the feet of Muslims and every mighty empire was smashed by their blow. Their unity brought them to zenith. They had surely understood the real meaning of Islamic brotherhood as Holy Quran says:

"And hold fast, altogether, the rope of Allah (which He stretches out for you) and be not divided amongst yourselves." (Al-e-Imran; Ayah: 103)

Therefore, Muslims of those times were always cemented together by this bond of Islam. Muslims were like a single body whose one organ in pain made all other organs restless and the pain was felt and responded to by all other parts. The Holy Prophet (PBUH) said:

"The Muslim society is like a body in respect of mutual love and sympathy, if a limb in the body suffers pain, the whole body responds to it by sleeplessness and fever."

However, the real unity was soon discovered by intriguers and hypocrites and the same unity was exploited cleverly and then gradually but steadily, Muslims reached the stage where they are today. This was just because they had forgotten what Holy Quran had said:

"Obey Allah and His Messenger and do not quarrel among yourselves; lest you lose heart and your momentum disappears." (Al-Anfal; Ayah: 46)

The Muslim Ummah held so tightly together in its early days now started to quarrel on small differences as hypocrites reminded them of the pre-Islamic tribal enmities. They worked silently aided by the malicious Jews who are always at the top of the list of conspirators against Islam. Allegations rose against the caliph Hazrat Usman (RA) from the rebel (hypocrite) group but these were answered logically to silent all. But then another scheme was plotted and the caliph was besieged in his house. One unfortunate day, the intriguers entered the house forcefully and Hazrat Usman (RA) was martyred on18th Zil Hajj 35 AH. A movement asking the new caliph Hazrat Ali (RA) for the revenge of Hazrat Usman (RA) was launched by Hazrat Aisha (RA), Hazrat Talha (RA) and Hazrat Zubair (RA). People feared of a battle between the two parties but just when peace prevailed once again by logical discussions between them, the intriguers rose again and their scheme brought about the first civil war of Islam, the Battle of Camel between Hazrat Aisha (RA) and Hazrat Ali (RA). None of the two was on the wrong side but the real victors were, obviously, the conspirators! They had won! They had made the mighty Islamic unity to be tumbled by the very first blow of 'division'. It was the first crack in the building of Islamic brotherhood and paved the way for further damages.

Then the first sect, the Kharijites appeared. Soon the enemy was putting in all energies of intrigues and then they had found the weak point. The holy post of caliphate then converted to kingship inherited to family successors. The tragedy of Karbala was what followed all this and the unity was shattered into pieces. Soon sects arose with full zeal and the mighty Muslim Ummah got divided into isolate islands. Different caliph dynasties came like the Umayyads, Abbasids, Fatimids and many more. Muslims had transformed into Shias, Sunnis and many other sectarian groups with the passage of time. The enemy had cunningly broken the Islamic bond of unity and had found the time to strike. With no more strong uniting forces, the whole Muslim empire was easily broken into pieces by one mere blow. Finally, caliphate, the last symbol of Muslim unity was also abolished after World War I and despite being the best nation from all aspects, the Muslim Ummah stands where it does.

Hence, with the Muslim Ummah divided into states and 'nations', the enemy had won in isolating the groups and even making them bitter enemies of each other. America then came forth as the new super power. Aided financially and also with conspiracies from the Jews they set to take 'revenge' from Muslims. A revenge for all utterly humiliating defeats the Christian world had faced at the hands of Muslims. With the whole Ummah as a body, the same Christians and Jews, even united, could never defeat them as is seen from the historic battles. But now, America is cunningly controlling almost the whole of the Islamic world. The Muslims are nearly the sole suppliers of mineral oil, the greatest and most expensive commodity, to the whole western world and the same oil is used by America to run its nation, earn dollars, and then pour these dollars into Israel's hands to continue the ruthless massacre of innocent Palestinian Muslims. The USA itself carries the blood of millions of Iraqi and Afghan Muslims directly and millions of others indirectly. The roads of these countries turn red with innocent Muslim blood but American brutality has no end as the ravage still continues. Moreover, India has also left no limit to cross in carrying out the same havoc in Kashmir and Muslims lay helplessly there as well.

Figure 22: Palestinian Muslim martyrs, Indian soldiers torturing innocent Kashmiri civilian Muslims, American 'peacefulness' revealed in Afghanistan

But the hilarious aspect is that the same two countries (America and India) are at the top of the list in claiming their innocuous victims, the Muslims, to be the real terrorists and a danger to world peace! However, to sum up, the difference between the two eras can be understood by the fact that with a united Muslim 'nation', a 17 year old Muhammad bin Qasim conquered the whole of the Sindh kingdom and defeated numerous Hindu Rajas merely on the call of a captivated Muslim sister. But now, with numerous Muslim 'nations' not a single son of Islam is courageous enough to respond to his Muslim sister Aafia Siddiqui's call.

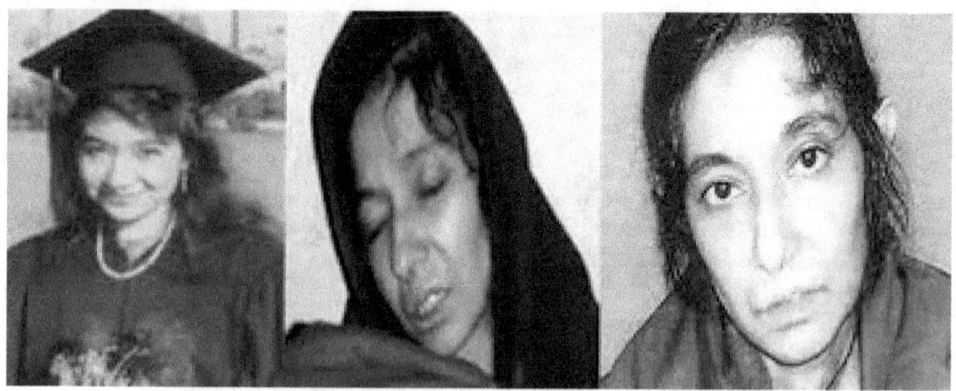

Figure 23: Dr. Aafia Siddiqui Over the Years

This is truly shameful!

Now that was the historic part and I shared many of the past memories that we have as a nation. But my brothers and sisters! Preserving the past is very important but only as long as it is used as a lesson for the future. Therefore, our story of glory with unity and downfall without unity teaches us that we have to be united once again at every cost! Iqbal said:

یہی مقصودِ فطرت ہے، یہی رمزِ مسلمانی
اُخوّت کی جہاں گیری، محبّت کی فراوانی

بُتانِ رنگ و خوں کو توڑ کر ملّت میں گم ہوجا
نہ تُورانی رہے باقی، نہ ایرانی نہ افغانی

Translation:

*(This is the destiny of nature, this is the secret of Islam_*

World-wide brotherhood, an abundance of love!

Break the idols of color and blood and become lost in the community

Let neither Turanians nor Iranians or Afghanis remain.)

The first step towards this unity is the shunning of sectarian division. We all are Muslims and believe in the basics of Islam so why should we fight on the numerous meanings the same ayah can give. Have we forgotten what Holy Quran had said about sectarian division? Let us see what it says to us:

"And for those who divided their religion and became sects_ you have nothing to do with them. Their case rests with God; then He will tell them what they used to do." (Al-An'am; Ayah: 159)

As we should be thinking of changing the whole world but always starting from our own self so there is an individual change needed, at least from our side. So there are two easy steps for our individual progress in this aspect: firstly, we should rely on the ayahs of Holy Quran which are 'Muhkamat' and define clear commandments about what to do and what not to do, rather than trying to reach deep meanings of other ayahs called the 'Mutashabihat' which have various meanings. In this way we can lead simple happy Islamic life abiding by all rules Allah has clearly jotted down for us. Not surprisingly, the Holy Quran has already told well in detail about this point as well. It says:

"It is He who revealed to you the Book. Some of its verses are definitive (Muhkamat); they are the foundation of the Book, the others are unspecific (Mutashabihat; can lead to more than one meanings). As for those whose hearts is deviation, they follow the unspecific part, seeking descent, and seeking to desire an interpretation. But none knows except Allah and those firmly rooted in knowledge say: 'We believe in it; all is

from our Lord.' But none recollects except those with understanding."
(Al-e-Imran; Ayah: 7)

Secondly, if we find someone who thinks contrary to us on a religious issue we have to respect his views, listen tolerably to all his logics and then kindly try to tell him our reasons. This peaceful but rational discussion would either lead to us accepting fully or a part of his views or vice versa. But if such does not happen, instead of going into harsh remarks, we should quit the discussion declaring that Allah knows better. These two steps are, in my thinking, the easiest way to eradicate sectarian division. As we know that the Muhkamats are surely believed in the same way by all sects and they are the Mutashabihat whose various meanings create differences. But we should never forget that religious tolerance has always been the distinctive quality of Muslims and we have to preserve it at any cost. We are the fresh upcoming generation and with us adapting such an attitude, we can easily eradicate sectarian quarrels and lifelong cold-wars.

Then comes the promotion of Islamic unity beyond the manmade barriers of countries and states. Although the Organization of the Islamic Conference (OIC) is working by providing a forum for representatives from all member Muslim countries to discuss difficulties and religious issues but, by all means, more is required.

Figure 24: The OIC logo

Muslim countries do help each other with enthusiasm in all times of need but the pity is the havoc which occurred and is still taking place in Palestine, Iraq, Afghanistan, Kashmir and more recently, in Burma but these Muslim 'countries' could not do a thing to stop it. Although the merging of all Muslim states into one single state seems impossible but at least, we should have the same friends and foes. We have to make ourselves firm enough to never repeat the mistake of the Gulf War and nor should we ever do anything like the blunder that Musharraf did by giving away Pakistani military posts to America to be used against a Muslim neighbor country (Afghanistan). We do need unity for another 'Rise of Islam'. Iqbal said:

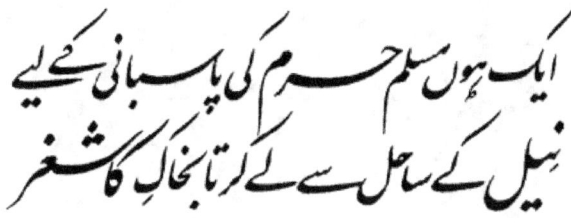

(*Translation:*

May the Muslims unite in watching over the shrine,

From the banks of Nile to the deserts of Kashghar.)

Now let us come to our unity at a different but closely linked perspective_ our unity as the Pakistani nation which can be understood by what Quaid said:

"We are now all Pakistanis_ not Baluchis, Pathans, Sindhis, Bengalis, Punjabis and so on_ and as Pakistanis we must feel, behave and act, and we should be proud to be known as Pakistanis and nothing else." (Quaid in his address on 15th June, 1948)

Being the youth of the first nuclear power of the Islamic world, it is inevitable for us to understand and apply this unity upon us. I would hence give you a fully detailed logical justification for this argument of mine. Just assume and imagine......

Imagine if we did not have Baluchistan with us. Can you think of the loss it could have brought about for us and how important are the Baluchi brothers for the integrity and honor of the country? Baluchistan, the land of deserts, is the place where great people live in a climate almost unbearable for people like us.

Figure 25: Baluchistan, The Land of Great People

The economic and mineral wealth of Baluchistan is just unimaginable. The Sui gas-field alone fulfills almost half of the country's gas requirements. The Saindak Copper Gold Project can supply us the precious gold. There are other innumerable mineral resources in Baluchistan which have been extensively identified by geologists world-wide but unfortunately, no heed has been paid by the governments up-to-date. Moreover, Gwadar port can provide a gateway to numerous mighty economic benefits. The fishing industry of Baluchistan provides some of the best varieties of seafood. Fruit production and livestock transhumance further increases the importance. Furthermore, the Baluchis provide a great workforce for mining work and other small-scale industries. So, it is proved that we can never live without Baluchistan.

Now imagine the same for Sindh. Sindh, the home for Indus Valley Civilization and the gateway for Islam in the sub-continent, is our pride. Even Karachi alone possesses an undeniable importance. It is the 'Industrial Hub' of the country and is also our greatest city with its importance further increased by its natural warm water harbor. Jinnah Terminal Karachi connects the East with the West due to its location. Moreover, it is the birth, as well as the resting place, of our great Quaid. No doubt, it is Sindh which contains the Thar coal-field, the greatest one of the whole Pakistan carrying coal worth the oil-fields of the Gulf States. Sindh contains Indus River whose tributaries provide water to the whole nation. This province is also the second largest agricultural producer of the country.

Figure 26: Sindh

So, the Sindhis with their beautiful culture and praiseworthy nature are surely our brothers and they do have their full share in contributing for the prosperity of the nation. And it is proved that we can definitely not live without Sindh either.

Then comes the land of the scrupulously exalted Pathans, the Khyber Pakhtunkhwa. The diligent, upstanding and proud Pathans themselves are the real beauty of this province with the people as strong as their faith and emotions. Amongst them are the extraordinarily free tribal people whose valor did not even allow the British to conquer their area or enslave them. Their bravery is always super and conduct admirable. Furthermore, the Khyber Pakhtunkhwa (KPK) gives us much of the foreign exchange earnings through tourism. Its beautiful landscape and agricultural advantages further add the importance of this area.

Figure 27: The beautiful Nathia Gali, KPK

The historic city of Peshawar and the important Khyber Pass are also an asset for the nation. Hence, this region can not be neglected and so, we can not live without the Pathans and their Khyber Pakhtunkhwa.

Now imagine a lack of the province of Punjab, the land of the five rivers and the abode for the diligent farmers and agriculturists.

The five rivers of Punjab are the biggest rivers of Pakistan and provide agricultural water, as well as electricity through the Hydel Power Plants, to the whole country. This area gives the greatest agricultural output with its fertile plains and beautiful doabs and plateaus. The staple food of Pakistan, wheat, is supplied almost solely by this province. Industrial activities are at their climax in this province as educational sector is also served the best over here. The historic cities of Lahore and Multan sum up to the already irresistible significance.

Due to this importance, the population is highest here and Punjabis provide the greatest amount of active workforce to the nation. So..... can Pakistanis live without Punjab? Obviously not.

Then comes the tough but all beautiful Gilgit Baltistan which lies amidst the towering peaks of the junction of the two greatest mountain ranges of the world, the Karakoram Range and the Himalayas. This area provides Pakistan with its mighty mountains and tourism benefits with its importance increased by the gigantic K-2 and the frozen Siachen. Our brave soldiers give up the comforts of a normal life to live in the terribly hostile climate of this area only because we can not live without Gilgit Baltistan either.

Figure 28: The Siachen Glacier

Last but never the least, are the ones who sacrificed their 'everything' for Pakistan and then left their entire lives along with the loved ones behind to serve Pakistan, the 'Muhajirs'. They were surely the ones who gave the martyr blood of all their dearest ones only for drawing the Eastern boundary of Pakistan. All of us Pakistani people were granted the blessing of freedom in the form of Pakistan and the people who paid the cost of that freedom were these Muhajirs. At that time, their love for Pakistan was so great that they saw their kin die in agony in front of their eyes and yet when they crossed the borders of Pakistan after being fully devastated in every manner, they forgot all that and did nothing except an unbelievable thanksgiving prostration over the soil recently irrigated so extensively by the blood of their nearest dearest ones. Today, they are an integral part of the Pakistani nation and are the reminders of the sacrifices given for freedom! They are our pride and we cannot survive if we neglect what they did for all of us.

Then it is Kashmir as well which can never be replaced by anything else in terms of importance. But firstly we need an inner unity amongst our existing provinces and only then we would be able to back our Kashmiri brothers in their fight for freedom.

So, think about it yourself now. Could Pakistan be so wealthy (naturally), beautiful or even existent if only a single part from all these would have been missing? This is the importance each and every Pakistani deserves, so why don't we give this significance and regard to everyone? We have to realise that every Pakistani is an equally inevitable part of the nation. We have to declare that every single one of us is a Baluchi, Sindhi, Punjabi, Pathan, Muhajir as well as a Kashmiri because every single one of us is Pakistan and Pakistan is not complete without either of its parts. This recognition of honor is obviously the first step to an increased national unity. As Iqbal says:

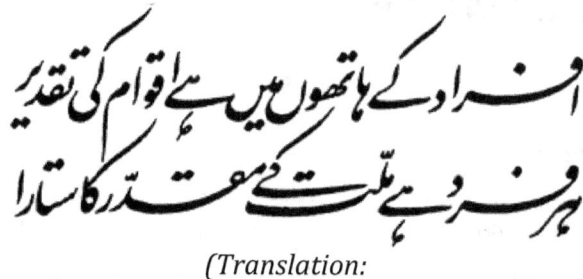

(Translation:

Fortunes of states in individual prowess ripen,

Each man one star of their ascendant (Destiny).)

Enemies always try out cunning schemes whenever they fail to destroy a nation in a face-to-face combat. Same is the situation with us today and same was the almost successful method implied upon the whole

Muslim Ummah and this 'method' shattered the Ummah into pieces. It is an open plot by the enemies of Islam and Pakistan in the form of traitors which disguise themselves as honest, local and humble 'leaders'. They are seen talking about many unnecessary limits of provincial autonomies reminding simple local people of their long forgotten grievances just in order to inculcate a feeling of malice against other provinces. Even a slight injustice is then highlighted and exaggerated to provoke enmities between two Pakistani brothers. On the other hand, other traitors sit comfortably in the parliament and intentionally maintain a differentiating behavior between two provinces to hold up the jealousy and hence, they deliberately cause the injustice which leads to deeper misunderstandings. So why have we, local people, always been be-fooled by these traitors and we continue to fight a cold war just because of their mischief. Simple is that; they are not the local people of a province who do injustice to another province so why are the local people of that province hated by others for a lack of equality in shares? This has to stop!

But nevertheless, I am sure that today we, the new generation, are not fools to be deceived by the traitors and treated in the same way over and over again. There is a grave need for us, the upcoming youth of Pakistan, to realize the importance of national unity in terms of experience with what has already happened to the Muslim Ummah, and then recognizing every province, every region and eventually, every individual of Pakistan as an equally integral part of the nation. This would easily root out all grievances, enmities and of course, all enemy intrigues focused so keenly on our unity. As a result, justice, healthy relationships, brotherhood, mutual love and unity would soon prevail Insha Allah! The need however, is just to realize that it is a perfectly proven truth that:

"United we stand, divided we fall!"

Chapter 7. The Cause Of Independence

It was a time during the reign of Brahmins over India before the advent of Islam here. People were busy shopping earnestly in a crowded marketplace. Buying and selling with full enthusiasm was at its climax and noisy arguments could be heard when all of a sudden, a small bell was heard ringing at a distance! And chaos ensued. It instantly seemed that the whole situation of calm and quiet was reversed as dropping everything they had, the people started running here and there searching frantically for a hideout. They were so terrified by the sound of the bell that those which could not find a hiding place just turned their backs towards the path, tightly closed their eyes and pushed their fingers in their ears. The peace of the marketplace had been converted so efficiently into a perfect mayhem by just a bell....

By now you all would have been convinced that the reason for the sudden fuss would be a thunderstorm warning or some army of enemy raiders of even some dangerous mighty wild monster approaching. But alas! what emerged as the cause of the ringing bell was neither a calamity nor a bandit group. Rather, those people were actually creating such a mess and were running merely from a feeble old man wearing tattered clothes, holding a stick with a small bell hanging on it and having a pitiful sigh on his face. Yes! He was the reason for all that. But do you know the reason? It was just because he was one of the 'untouchable people', belonging to the 'chandala' or 'achuta' caste of India. Brahmins ran from the old man, shut their eyes and ears and stood motionlessly until the man with the bell vanished in the dust. This was the social and economic boycott of the achutas and the Brahmin brutality on the local people!

But this was not all! Although a complete boycott was enough to push a community into the well of doom but still it was not all. Those people were not allowed to stand or sit or even dream to intermarry with the Brahmins. Their shadow was devastating for the 'Brahminism' of

Brahmins and even a sight or voice of them was considered a seriously bad omen. They could not perform any ritual even of Hinduism or participate in any religious ceremony. They were practically called the 'noseless' and the 'godless' people. They were inhumanely beaten, gunned, burnt alive or even raped to tell them their status; which was that they were the 'untouchable'. Their genocide in many areas was a common thing. They were bound to live always in the outskirts where no one ever came and even had to hold a bell so that the Brahmins would be warned of their presence and could take precautions before a mere sight of them..... Brutality and cruelty summed up with injustice had no limit, no end!

Most of you would be thinking of the relevance of all this with the topic. This factual account was only meant to give you a picture of Hindu nature and to provide you a comparison_ a real comparison of their behavior towards these people and then towards the local Muslims during the unforgettable Hindu rule over Muslims in the sub-continent from 1937-1939. This rule enhanced all other reasons for fighting for freedom and hence it is the greatest cause to trigger the Pakistan Movement which formally started merely three months after the rule ended.....

Figure 30: Minar.e.Pakistan

The 1937 elections were held under the proposals of the Government of India Act 1935 enforced by the British. The Muslim League, not being properly organized or experienced could not manage to win even in Muslim majority areas and Congress formed ministries in 8 out of 11 provinces. However, the Congress claim of representing 95% of Indian population could not be proved either. Congress leaders wanted to rule without any strict British interference and hence delayed the formation of government. The British viceroy Lord Linlithgow gave them this safeguard as well and Congress took over to repeat their cruelties over the potentially weaker nations. But this time they were not 'achutas'.... They were the Muslims, practically a numerical minority in India.

This was a historic introduction for you all. I want you to focus now on the ravage which had started the day Congress took over. From a common Hindu to the government itself, everyone was out to destroy Muslim culture, recognition, differentiation and then eventually to expel local Muslims from their 'Hindustan'. As a start, building a new mosque and even the proclamation of 'adhaan' was prohibited in many areas and whoever broke the law was deliberately murdered by Hindu extremists. Cow slaughtering was a crime with death as the only penalty. During prayer times, noisy processions were arranged near mosques to disturb Muslims to the extreme limit. Then to cross all limits, pigs were thrown into mosques when Muslims were busy in prayers. There were riots which always followed such incidents and whenever a case about it was taken up by a victim Muslim, the courts always ruled in favor of Hindus and Muslims were thrown behind the bars. Their houses and property was set on fire and they were killed whenever the Hindus wanted so. Every right of Muslims to defend themselves or to even live peacefully with their religion was completely confiscated in this tyranny.

But these were mere disorganized attempts from local Hindus to erase Muslim culture. But the savage acts were carried out in a better 'organized' way by the Congress government itself.

Figure 30: The main Congress leadership

Hindi with Deva Nagri script was made official language and Urdu with Persian script was even taken down from its original ranking of second official language. To hunt Muslim feelings, a Hindu extremist song called 'Bande Matram' which encouraged the eradication of Islam and the expulsion of Muslims was officially made the national anthem (it was necessary to sing it in the whole country at start of every official day).

Then even the sector of education was not spared. Rather, it was given a keen focus as Muslims were becoming more and more aware day by day. Therefore, 'Wardha Scheme' was launched excluding any Islamic religious education from the curriculum and adding the lessons of cotton spinning instead. The Hindus' so called 'superiority' over Muslims was highlighted in a completely exaggerated manner and Muslim culture and religion was insulted in front of young innocent Muslim children. Sadly enough, children from all religions were forcefully made to bow in front of a portrait of Gandhi hung in all schools. But Hindus were not satisfied by this! Another plan called the 'Vidhya Mandir' scheme was introduced to aid the Wardha Scheme. Schools were built in their structure and formation resembling Hindu 'mandirs' (temples) and the teachers were Hindu priests cunningly deviating the minds of Muslim children from Islam to Hinduism. The result was obvious as planned by Congress! Nearly all Muslims withdrew their children from schools and Muslim education went into a serious decline.

During all this havoc, the Muslim League tried hard to make matters better for the Muslims with Quaid trying severely to convince the Congress leaders to form a coalition government at least in Muslim majority provinces. But he was rebuked in return by the wild brutes sitting in the Parliaments. 'Pirpur Report' was made by Muslim League providing a summary of the extreme injustice done towards Muslims but Congress government paid no heed to this as well.

Figure 31: Muslim League leadership in those days

Hence, after that, two paths were identified by the Hindus themselves for two distinct nations. Muslims were truly convinced that if Hindus were so preposterous under the British so when once the British would have left, their ruthlessness could rise to an unimaginable extent. Although, finally, after two years of mass annihilation the Congress ministries resigned in protest to British demand for India to help them in warfare. Hence, on 22 December 1939, Muslims all over India celebrated the 'Day of Deliverance' under the Muslim League's flag. It was now confirmed that neither the British nor the Hindus were trustworthy and so Muslims had to find a way to live on their own.

After reading this detailed account, most of you would have been convinced that this rule was the biggest reason for Pakistan being so crucial. However, there were many other reasons as well but they all were also aroused to their fullest only after this rule. One such reason was the past having comparatively minor grievances for Muslims at the hands of Congress. I would surely like to explain this point to you as well just to make you clear that there were solid logical reasons behind the all difficult 'fight for Pakistan' and hence, to reassure you that the existence of Pakistan is never an unnecessary aspect of our lives.

We all know that Congress was formed in 1885 aiming to form a political representative body for all Indians but it soon turned out to be a Hindu party. The first proof came in 1905 when Bengal was partitioned by the British. But Congress reaction was uncouth! They knew that this partition would give Muslims an extra Muslim majority province and hence, they started mass strikes headed by Congress leaders saying that Indian unity was in danger and this eventually led to the British reversing the partition. This propaganda moved Muslims to think that they needed their own representative party severely and hence Muslim League was founded in 1906. Then Muhammad Ali Jinnah (the Great Quaid) appeared as a member of both Congress and Muslim League. He, being called the 'Ambassador of Hindu-Muslim unity' in those days, proposed a Lucknow pact between the parties to reach an agreement. Although Congress temporarily agreed to Muslim demands but when time came for practicality, they returned to their original stance and denied everything with full deceit.

Another betrayal came with the Khilafat Movement. This was a movement meant solely for Muslims and Congress had nothing to do with it. But, to cheat Muslims, Mr. Gandhi jumped into the mess and emerged as the new leader of the movement of preservation of the 'Muslim' caliph. Quaid had, by now, deeply realized the nature of Congress and hence he warned Muslims also from being befooled but their enthusiasm was not to be restricted. However, the foresight of Quaid soon proved to be a reality when at the peak of all protests, campaigns and delegations, Gandhi suddenly called off the non-cooperation movement in 1922 and eventually the Khilafat Movement also died away.

Then came the Nehru Report in 1928 with all its points against Muslim interests and clearly implementing a Hindu dominion over the sub-continent.

Figure 32: Pandit Motilal Nehru (the one to present the 'Nehru Report')

Quaid proposed some amendments to be done but after being heckled by Congress leaders, he was disappointed and any trust leftover for Congress soon disintegrated. Then the Round Table Conferences of 1930, 1931 and 1932 further marked the parting of ways when Gandhi clearly denied even to recognize the minority problem of Muslims in the sub-continent. After all these experiences and apathetic behavior by Congress, the Congress rule of 1937-1939 proved to be the last nail in the coffin of any hope of better relations between Muslims and Hindus and hence, Hindus themselves made Pakistan inevitable.

Now, my brothers and sisters, you all can easily guess that in such situations, Muslims were moved to think that if British would leave India simply hoping it to sort out its mess itself, it would obviously lead to Muslims permanently becoming lifelong slaves of the Hindu majority. The biggest proof was the Congress rule itself. Now, without any doubt, the Hindus of India wanted to rule over Muslims just as they had done on the numerical minority of seemingly weak people, the 'achutas'. But they had forgotten that a true Muslim can never be suppressed by force. The case with Muslims was totally different because they had previously been the rulers of the same sub-continent for nearly a thousand years. A Hindu dominion over Muslims was never acceptable to for our proud ancestors. How could they ever accept their generations, that means us, to lead lives like or even worse than those who lived under the Hindu tyranny? Muslims had once been the rulers and now them becoming enslaved to one after another nation was not at all acceptable.

Another aspect was the Hindu thought declaring that the expulsion of Muslims was necessary in order to create a true 'Hindustan'. Rather, Muslims were another local nation who had a truly justified right to live freely and that could never ever seem to be a reality under the overwhelming Hindu majority. When Muslims ruled over India, if Islam would have ever been spread by force or by sword, there could never have been any Hindu 'majority' problem in the first place and hence, there wouldn't even have been any need for the 'Pakistan Movement'. This explains that Islam never spread by force nor were all Muslims Arabs who migrated to India. Rather, Islam was a spiritual attainment gained by the locals who were inspired by the behavior and character of Arab Muslim merchants. Hence, any question of Muslim expulsion became utterly pointless. Muslims belonged to the same land and upheld the same rights which were never to be safeguarded by Hindus under Congress.

In addition to all these reasons, Muslim dignity and pride was another factor paving the way for them to demand independence. It is a common fact known by all of us that a true Muslim never accepts the slavery of anyone except Allah. Then the slavery of Hindus could be an even greater insult so who of our ancestors could accept that? Muslims are born to be leaders and not slaves of the world. The need was just to prove it and hats off to those who proved it in the form of an 'unbelievably miraculous Pakistan'. Iqbal calls this sense of pride as 'Khudi' and says:

خودی کو نہ دے سیم و زر کے عوض نہیں شعلہ دیتے شرر کے عوض

(Translation:

Barter not thy selfhood for silver and gold;

Sell not a burning flame for a spark half-cold.)

Moreover, in Islamic terminology, fighting against an unjust ruler is the greatest Jihad and Muslims were, hence, performing this Jihad. The Holy Prophet (PBUH) had said:

"And hold against the hand of the unjust ruler, and force him to the truth strongly, or you have to limit him to the truth."

Now, my dear brothers and sisters, it has been logically proved to you that a 'Pakistan' was, by all means, inevitable for the survival of Islam in the sub-continent. This was an obvious answer to all those who say that the creation of Pakistan was only a waste of time, energy and blood and that Pakistan initiated the enmity between Hindus and Muslims. No! But Pakistan was a barrier, a safeguard for the Muslims of sub-continent. It was a self-owned home for them to lead their lives freely. Its walls were boundaries to protect Muslims from the brutality and the barbarity of Hindus. Anyhow..... Let us now come to the ideology of Pakistan which was to be made after whatever Congress and Hindus had done to Muslims. This ideology came to be known as the 'Two Nations Theory'......

This theory was put forth for the first time by the Father of the Pakistan Movement, Sir Syed Ahmad Khan. His foresight had already anticipated the result of the differences in the 'two nations' as he said in 1878:

"Now suppose that all English were to leave India then who could be the rulers of India? Is it possible that under these circumstances, the 'two nations'_ the Muslims and the Hindus_ could sit on the same throne and remain equal in power? Most certainly not. It is necessary that one of them should conquer the other and thrust it down. To hope that both could remain equal is to desire the impossible and the inconceivable."

This 'Two Nations Theory' was adopted later in forefront by the architect of Pakistan, Allama Iqbal as he said in December 1933 in an answer to Jawaharlal Nehru who was a staunch supporter of a united India:

"In conclusion, I must put a straightforward question to Jawaharlal Nehru, how is India's problem to be solved if the majority community will neither concede the minority of 80 million people, nor accept the award of a Third Party; but continue to talk of a kind of nationalism which works out only to its own benefit? This position can admit of only two alternatives. Either the Indian majority community will have to accept for itself the permanent position of an agent of British imperialism in the East or the country will have to be redistributed on a basis of religions, historical and cultural differences so as to do away with questions of electrorates and the communal problem in its present form."

However, Quaid took a firm footing on this theory only after the Congress rule when he said on March 22, 1940 at Lahore:

"It is extremely difficult to appreciate why our Hindu friends fail to understand the real nature of Islam and Hinduism. They are not religions in the strict sense of the word, but are, in fact, different and distinct social orders and it is a dream that the Hindus and Muslims can ever evolve a common nationality and this misconception of one Indian nation has troubles and will lead India to destruction if we fail to revise in our notions in time. The Hindus and Muslims belong to two different religious philosophies, social customs, literatures. They do not

intermarry nor interdine together and indeed they belong to two different civilizations which are based mainly on conflicting ideas and conceptions. Their aspects on life and of life are different. It is quite clear that Hindus and Muslims derive their inspiration from different sources of history. They have different epics, different heroes and different episodes. Very often the hero of one is the foe of the other and likewise, their victories and defeats overlap. To yoke together two such nations under a single state one as a numerical minority and other as a majority, must lead to growing discontent and final destruction of any fabrics that may be so built for the government of such a state."

Now, brothers and sisters, after reading everything about Congress tyranny, the eternal indifference and enmity of Hindus towards Muslims and after recognizing that Muslims rightly feared another slavery, can anyone of you disagree with what Iqbal and Quaid said? But even after a full detailed explanation of solid logics, it was the Congress which continued to deny this theory on the basis of one mere childish argument about which Gandhi wrote to Quaid-e-Azam on September 15, 1944:

"I find no parallel in history for a body of converts and their descendents claiming to be a nation apart from their parent stock. If India was one nation before the advent of Islam, it must remain one inspite of the change of faith of a very large body of her children."

However Quaid answered to this 'logic' magnificently to silent all. He wrote to Gandhi on19 September, 1944:

"We maintain and hold that Muslims and Hindus are two major nations by any definition or test of a nation. We are a nation of a hundred million and what is more, we are a nation with our own distinctive culture and civilization, language and literature, art and architecture, names and nomenclature, sense of values and proportion, legal laws and moral codes, customs and calendar, history and tradition, aptitudes and ambition. In short, we have our own distinctive outlook on life. By all canons of international law, we are a nation."

What are your views now? .... However, even if you put aside all what everyone said about this theory, it was in reality the religious discrimination reflecting in the Hindu and Congress behavior which paved the way to Muslims putting forth this theory. Their own differentiating behavior towards Hindus and Muslims made even a common Muslim think that they were a nation separate from Hindus. So Hindus themselves initiated the mere idea of a 'Two Nations Theory' hence leading to Pakistan.

So, although these were all the reasons why we needed Pakistan so badly, but they can never be the only reasons why Pakistan was created. Rather, there was and is still another 'group of reasons' known only to the 'Sustainer of the Worlds' who had started the preparations for a mighty Islamic state to be created in this area centuries ago when a seemingly unconcerned Muslim ship was unjustly captured by the ruler of Sindh calling in the Great Muhammad bin Qasim. However, what I personally know as an answer to the question "Why a 'Pakistan'?" is only that all these reasons for us needing Pakistan described so explicitly in this chapter still fall far too short in front of the statement:

"Pakistan was not created because 'we' needed Pakistan. Rather, Pakistan was created because the world needed 'us'."

Chapter 8. Cost Of Independence

I have told you so far about many things, different aspects and importance of identity, our relations with the history, the importance of unity and most recently, I told you about the reasons why we needed a separate homeland so desperately. But now, I would tell and prove that:

"To gain which is worth having, it may be necessary to lose everything else."

This chapter is an attempt to make you recall the 'cost of independence' which our forefathers had to pay for our freedom, and to tell you how they lost everything else to gain which was worth having and that was, 'Pakistan'!

It was obviously Quaid's leadership and determination which, summed up with Almighty's help and the Muslim nation's enthusiasm, granted us Pakistan but freedom always costs a lot and our freedom indeed cost too much! Many of you would have obviously heard of the problems our new born country had to face and some would also be knowing the sacrifices themselves, but here, the purpose is not knowledge. The real purpose is our reaction, our actions which would prove the dignity and self-respect that we possess. Now I would just request you to read the historic account very carefully and then if you are a true Pakistani or even a human being, do think about what the conclusion says…..

You have been told earlier on about the Hindu brutality on achutas and hence the nature of Hinduism has been explained to you. But now, in 1940s, they were facing a different nation_ the Muslims. This nation actually wanted a separate country which meant a considerable piece to be cut off from the 'territory of Hindus'. Now they were bound to be bamboozled, as this Muslim nation was neither to be defeated in wars nor suppressed by force like the achutas. They had indeed crushed

Hindu power under their feet several times and had ruled over the Hindus so their destruction was an impossible dream for Hindus. Keeping in mind all these facts, the Hindus were now on their way to try out the last option they had, and that was cunning deceits. Hence, to aid them, Lord Louis Mountbatten had arrived in India on 22 March, 1947 to carry out the transfer of powers.

Figure 33: Louis Mountbatten

Now, unfortunately for the Muslims of India, Mountbatten admired Jawaharlal Nehru and the Labor government in Britain also supported Congress. But then, anyone can be moved to think that if his favors lay with the Congress manifesto, then why did he ever agree to a 'Pakistan'? The answer lies in what he recognized Pakistan to be. In his thought, 'Pakistan' was simply an unrealistic childish thought which would never be able to stand on its feet and would soon collapse. Hence, his master conspirator mind soon prepared a scheme to please the Hindus so much that they even actually appointed him as the new India's first governor general. The first and the deadliest part of his scheme came into visibility as the Radcliffe award.

The 3rd June Plan (put forth on June 3, 1947) had announced the formation of Pakistan and had given Sindh and Baluchistan to Pakistan. NWFP (today's Khyber Pakhtunkhwa) opted for Pakistan after a public referendum while Punjab and Bengal had to be partitioned into Muslim majority and Hindu majority areas. This was where a serious drama could be created. In the 3rd June Plan, some Muslim majority areas of Punjab between Sutlej and Beas had been given to India while River Sutlej was to be the natural boundary between the two countries. Gurdaspur, a whole Muslim majority district was to be a part of Pakistan according to the announced plan while the Muslim Assam district near Bengal had to join the Eastern Wing of Pakistan. But the main plot was to try to hide the real culprits in the smoke of haste and hence, the date for Indian Independence was brought forward from June 1948 to 15th August 1947 in the same 3rd June plan.

Now, I would tell you the truths behind the changing of the temporary boundaries of 3rd June plan into the charter of death for the millions of Muslims of Eastern Punjab and Kashmir and this charter was then named as the 'Radcliffe Award'. The initial boundaries of 3rd June plan were still not completely fair as many Muslim majority areas still lay in India but what the innocent Muslims could never anticipate was the extent to where the Hindu uncouthness could reach. Their heinousness could never rest on this. They needed blazes of fire burning away the Muslims, they needed Muslim blood to quench the thirst of Hindu inhumanity thickly covered by the veil of friendship and mercy for many ages. Their brutality needed freedom; a freedom from every limit, just to do what no one had ever done in the history of mankind. So, to finally accomplish their dreams, Sir Cyril Radcliffe landed his feet on the 'Bharat Dharti Mata'.

Figure 34: Cyril Radcliffe

And the power was finally handed over to two independent states, Pakistan and India, during the night between the 14th and 15th of August, 1947. The very first bomb on the confidence of Pakistan was thrown when Radcliffe award was announced on 17th of August, 1947. The natural boundary of Sutlej had been further constricted instead of any expected relaxation and so, the new natural boundary was now River Ravi. Another blow was stricken, when the whole Gurdaspur district was announced as a part of India. Ferozepur, Batala, Amritsar, Ajnalain, Zira and Jullundar were other main Muslim majority areas given ruthlessly to India. Moreover, Calcutta, the backbone of Bengal, was given to India even when it had many areas of clear Muslim majority. But by drawing this single line, Radcliffe and Mountbatten had done everything.

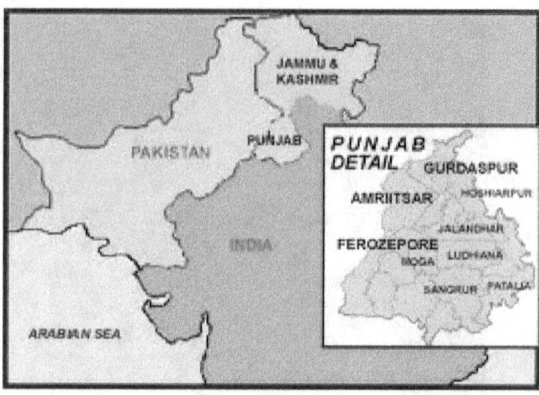

Figure 35: Radcliffe Award

Firstly, the most fertile regions of Punjab were handed over to India along with all important head works of the rivers of Punjab allowing India to tease Pakistan in any way it liked and the water disputes continuing up-to-date became inevitable. Secondly, they had deprived Pakistan of the industries and the developed port of Calcutta, and hence, also of the only military depot in Bengal was also snatched. This badly affected the economy as well as the military strength of the new born Pakistan. Thirdly, India wanted all three of the major princely states namely Hyderabad (Deccan), Junagadh and Kashmir. Therefore, it was necessary to eradicate Muslim Gurdaspur from India's pathway to Kashmir so to lead to an everlasting enmity between the two states over Kashmir.

However, the reason greatest of all was to carry out a common massacre of the Muslims of Eastern Punjab and then to give them no refuge nearby. For those people, crossing the River Ravi to reach their dreamland was in itself an almost impossible task to accomplish. Furthermore, the sudden influx of more than 10 million homeless, penniless and panic-stricken people into a new born country was just enough to shake its foundations violently. And then....... Can you just imagine what happened next? No! No one in this whole world with a heart can imagine the incidents which followed this unjust boundary line. The unmatched atrocities carried out on the Eastern side of the Punjab border and the utter helplessness made inevitable on the other is just enough to make a person even with the hardest heart of all to cry! To cry out loud and to ask the sky why it was silent when all this happened? And the sky was truly silent or perhaps it was speechless and even emotionless on seeing what it had never seen before. The limit of human barbarity was just crossed by the inhumane Sikhs of Punjab.

The local Muslims of the areas joined in Pakistan by the 3rd June plan held thanksgiving processions like all other Pakistanis at the night of 14th of August, 1947.

Figure 36: The upheld flag of Pakistan

 They had even fixed Pakistani flags on their homes and prostrated in front of the Almighty for granting them an independent, separate, Muslim homeland. But the truth was unraveled two days after independence when boundary commission announced its report. Prior to that, everything had been cunningly pre-planned. All the Muslims, even those of local villages had been unarmed saying that the government anticipated mischief from the Muslims' side. But once the boundary was announced, the atrocity had been made free of every limit or restriction and then, organized attacks from local Sikh groups started. Nearly all the Muslim militants or policemen, even constables, were first court-martialled and then gunned to death to eliminate every single armed support for the Muslims of Eastern Punjab. The real havoc was about to start!

On 15th of August, the Sikhs and Hindus of the same Muslim majority areas had feared mischief from their Muslim neighbors but they did nothing. In fact, some of them even guarded the houses of their neighbor non-Muslims. But in turn, they were betrayed! ……. Yes! And indeed, they were punished for putting their trust with the British, Hindus and the Sikhs. The Sikhs gathered on from the local areas just after the Radcliffe award was announced. They then armed themselves fully to start assaults on local innocuous unarmed Muslims. The Sikhs had already been told by the Hindus that they can only create their homeland 'Khalistan' by eliminating Muslims from the area given to them. They easily besieged village after village and killed each and every Muslim ruthlessly followed by the turning of a living village into blazes of brutal fire. But being unprotected could never become the reason for a Muslim to become a coward and none of them died a humiliating death because they fought. They fought till their last breath with spears, swords and bricks compared to all kinds of modern rifles and hand grenades. Even machine guns and army tanks were supplied where the unarmed 'resistance' was greater. But the most painful situation of all was when the throats of local Muslim peasants were cut by their own neighbors who were once guarded by the same Muslims. The young boys were brutally slaughtered and their corpses disfigured. Any Muslim who dared to kill any of the Sikhs was murdered most cruelly with his corpse then cut into a thousand pieces in front of all his family members tied at a distance.

Then the barbarity reached its climax and humanity screamed out of helplessness when young innocent Muslim girls were tortured in front of the eyes of their fathers tied nearby. They were tortured and dishonored until the last breath was taken out from their innocent beings. And each and every Muslim woman was dishonored that day. Then the merciless sky even perceived many Muslim girls and women running frantically. But they ran not for life! Rather, they ran for an honorable death. Many fortunate ones from them were able to commit suicide but those who were captured received an eternal disgrace…. A lifelong shameful slavery! Only a woman understands what any other woman could have felt in a certain situation but I have to declare that I am unable to even think about what those hundreds of Muslim women would have felt when they were tied and dragged on the streets of Amritsar in front of a jeering crowd; naked.

The fate of Muslim children and infants can never be explained in words. You can just understand that they were thrown up high in air and spear shooting and sword fighting was practiced as parts of flesh were slowly separated from their infant beings. All this was done in front of their mothers who could just do nothing but to cry out helplessly. I am out of words..

And yet, yet they loved Pakistan; loved it with every beat of their hearts.

In his own book, 'The other side of silence', an Indian author Harjit wrote:

"I cannot explain it, but one day our entire village took off to a nearby village on a killing spree. We simply went mad. And it has cost me 50 years of remorse, of sleepless nights_ I cannot forget the faces of those we killed."

Finally, it was over! No, but I should say that finally the first part of Mountbatten's scheme was over. Heaps of carcasses of Muslims lay everywhere in the Eastern Punjab and the Assam district near Bengal and the Muslim blood was now in abundance with every thirst for this blood quenched. Muslim villages and whole districts were heaps of debris and there were ashes of sweet homes everywhere. The paradise was now an unperceivable hell, a mixture of fire and blood! And what followed all this was the migration itself.

*Figure 37: Refugees craving to reach their
'Dreamland', Pakistan*

Millions of refugees arrived Pakistan with an even greater number of
them killed along the way. Trains filled with Muslim corpses reaching
Pakistan was now a common scene. Those coming from Eastern
Punjab were looted for the umpteenth time when they finally reached
Pakistan, half-mad with fear. And they had good reason to be mad. But,
my brothers and sisters, none of you can imagine what these calamity-
stricken people actually did when they entered the borders of
Pakistan. All of them only let out a soft cry and fell out in a
"thanksgiving" prostration. Many of them took out the soil of the
dearest homeland and kissed it frantically. They had reached their
destiny, the land of their dreams, their own Pakistan for which they
had sacrificed too much of their possessions!

I know all of you would be wondering about the role of Pakistan and
Quaid-e-Azam when all this happened. Quaid protested fully to the
Radcliffe award as his foresight had already anticipated what was to
follow. But hats off to Mountbatten! ..... He just threatened our Quaid
that as powers had already been transferred and so there would be
simply no Pakistan if these boundaries were not accepted.
Furthermore, he also put the blame of all ravages in Eastern Punjab
and Western Bengal as well on our Quaid saying that he had caused all
the 'riots' by forming a Pakistan! Now, the locals of Pakistan were
obviously outraged when they heard of the atrocities carried out on

Muslims in Eastern Punjab, Hyderabad (Deccan), Junagadh and Western Bengal. But thanks to the organizers of the boundary lines that these Pakistani Muslims did not even have a single area of considerable Hindu or Sikh population to take even the slightest of the revenge. But to add to the already unparalleled destruction, the non-Muslim migrants from Pakistan had actually started an "aided" massacre of local Muslim residents in Delhi. All this was happening and Gandhi, Nehru and Mountbatten were telling the international media about how nothing had occurred except some occasional 'skirmishes' and 'peace' had been 'restored' after introducing a visa system for migrants. And while they said all this, they were surely standing in the Indian streets stained red everywhere with the blood of innocent Muslims. Hence, our Quaid had nothing left to do except to put a little confidence in the devastated people of his new born Pakistan by saying:

"We are in the midst of unparalleled difficulties and untold sufferings.....
The systematic massacre of defenseless and innocent people puts to
shame even the most heinous atrocities committed by the worst tyrants
known to history. We have been the victims of a deeply-laid and well-
planned conspiracy executed with utter disregard of the elementary
principles of honesty, chivalry and honor...... Do not be afraid of death.
Our religion teaches us always to be prepared for death. We should face
it bravely to save the honor of Pakistan and Islam. There is no better
salvation for a Muslim than the death of a martyr for a righteous cause."

Figure 38: Quaid listening to a refugee

I hope you all would have become fully aware of the real cost of our freedom and this Pakistan which our ancestors had to pay. After reading this chapter, if the value in your heart for your motherland has risen even over a single degree, I would surely think that Almighty has granted me a considerable success!

Now let us come to the conclusion and our joint response to all the facts covered in this chapter. I have told you everything now, all about the inner intrigues which the British and Hindus carried out in such a united way just to destroy our nation. Although we all know that our existence till now is the biggest proof of the failure of all their conspiracies against us. But does that mean that it is over? No! They would never give up as their enmity towards us is eternal. They are still busy designing and carrying out even more advanced plots against our integrity and sovereignty as the Pakistani nation. Their allies are now even more powerful and greater in number. Their attacks are even severer. So are we to perish at their hands? No! Wake up! Can we ever forget the helpless cries of millions of our sisters whose honors were smashed under the feet of the limitless Hindu barbarity, or those mothers whose infant babies were murdered slowly and painfully in front of their eyes, or those brothers who fought with a dauntless bravery even without the rarest resources, or those fathers whose daughters were dishonored to death in front of their own eyes? If this independence was too costly, obviously its maintenance would also be costly. Therefore, we have to be mentally and physically prepared for every conspiracy that rises and should be ready to sacrifice even more to retain this country for our future generations and for our Islam!

Chapter 9. The Meaning of Pakistan

The title set for this chapter would be regarded as a petty topic by almost every glancing eye because nearly all of us are aware of the explicit meaning of the 'word' Pakistan with its origins as well. But the purpose I intend is to make you aware of the 'real' meaning of Pakistan from all its possible aspects. The very first thing to understand here is that Pakistan is not at all merely a word nor is this only the name of a country or a nation. Rather, it is a 'term' with lots of meanings while all of them equally affecting our mode of thinking and code of life.

Starting from scratch, I would firstly tell you or more probably, remind you of the intellectual meaning of Pakistan. By searching for the meaning of merely the word out of the whole term, we come to know that the word 'Pakistan' belongs to the Persian language. 'Pak', a Persian word, means 'pure' while '-istan', another Persian word, means 'living place'. Therefore, the simple linguistic meaning becomes 'the pure living place'. But this book is meant more for application than knowledge. So, my dear brothers and sisters! Go into a little deeper sense of the same simple meaning just for a moment and try to apply it to practicality. Can we imagine the sort of country the founders of Pakistan intended to make by picking such a noble name? Obviously, it does not seem to have turned out to be like its name till now. But the reality is, that Pakistan is still the same pure land, he same 'pure living place' which our forefathers handed over to our nation but unfortunately, the dwellers of this pure land could not comply with the full essence of the name granted to our country!

Another beautiful meaning extracted from its linguistic structure, by Chauhdri Rehmat Ali, is an indication of the unity of the peoples of Pakistan. It says:

P..unjab

A..fghania (Khyber Pakhtun Khwa)

K..ashmir

I..*

S..indh

T..

A BaluchisTAN

N..

*Added for convenience in pronunciation.

Figure 39: Chauhdry Rehmat Ali, the one to propose the name 'Pakistan'

This meaning of Pakistan reflects the key importance of every part of our beloved country. An important point to note here is that Kashmir is an integral 'part of Pakistan' because it contains millions of Muslims suffering at the hands of the inhumane Hindus of India. I told you in the last chapter that a common border with Kashmir was deliberately given to India in order to provide Hindus a place to quench the thirst of their everlasting 'coward' barbarity and also to initiate differences with Pakistan. Most of us have actually forgotten the Kashmiri freedom fighters with an excuse of the increasing internal tensions. But beware! For it is, in reality, a trial to check our attachment and sensations for our fellow Muslims. Those who are tortured in Kashmir would surely get their reward from the Almighty but surely, we, as a nation have to prepare for the answer we are to give in order to satisfy the questioning eyes of our Kashmiri brothers on the Day of Resurrection.

This was all that could have been said about the explicit meaning of the 'word' Pakistan. But just imagine the time when this 'Pakistan' was created. At that time, these meanings were only restricted to the educated minority amongst all the Indian Muslims. Hence, not surprisingly, this was not the meaning which convinced a local, uneducated, Muslim peasant to sacrifice all his possessions for its cause! Rather, there was a deeper implicit meaning, a picture of Pakistan engraved in the heart of every Indian Muslim, whether educated or uneducated.

Figure 40: fighters for Pakistan

This picture was the real meaning for the freedom-fighters while the artists behind this 'pictorial meaning' comprised of the Muslim League leadership. For those illiterate people, Pakistan meant a shelter, a home and a protection barrier to guard them from every calamity.

They thought of Pakistan as their own homeland, in fact a dreamland, where they would be able to live freely with no chains of slavery, where no national laws could restrict them from performing their religious rituals, where they would be far away and protected from Hindu atrocity as well as from the British injustice, where all their basic rights would be respected, where prosperity and happiness would prevail and above all, where they would find a whole country 'of their own'. But, sadly enough, our earlier generations almost failed here as well in bringing this meaning into reality.

Then comes another extremely important meaning of the term 'Pakistan' which was held in the highest esteem by the founders of this country. This meaning can be completely understood by the slogan raised by every Indian Muslim at that time:

"Hindustan will have to be divided (partitioned)

Pakistan will have to be created

What is the 'meaning of Pakistan'?

There is no God but Allah!)"

This slogan and the meaning it has can fully eradicate every doubt about the relationship between Islam and Pakistan. The ideology of Pakistan was the 'Two Nations Theory' which comprised of the clear differentiating line between Hindus and Muslims. This country was meant for Muslims and for Islam. There is simply no other comprehendible purpose for the creation of Pakistan except the protection of Muslims and of Islam while all other defined purposes are surely the subordinates of this single cause. The 'Islamic Republic of Pakistan' had to be based firmly on Islam with each and every constitutional legislation finding its origins from the Quran, Hadis and Sunnah. Most importantly, the social laws comprising of the punishments for any violation of the social, moral or legal codes has to be based on the Quran. This is one of the major reasons for our nation being utterly unable to control its ever increasing crime-rate and this is the same reason for Saudi Arabia having such a low crime-rate as compared to the vulgar society of America. However, the judicial procedure of investigation and honest proof-finding should remain the same except a meager change in carrying out the punishments. Nevertheless, the laws have to be Islamic as the first step to bring Islam in its true essence in the community of our beloved Pakistan to bring this meaning into being. But then again, extremism is not Islam and likewise, carrying out clear cut instructions of the Holy Quran is NOT extremism!

However, apart from these meanings, there was still another meaning of the term 'Pakistan' at the time of its creation. This meaning of Pakistan was what its enemies understood. When the Pakistan Movement was started, 'Pakistan' for them, meant a childish, unrealistic dream. In fact, it were the Hindus who sarcastically gave the name 'Pakistan Resolution' to the original 'Lahore Resolution' of 23rd March, 1940. They could just not think beyond it. They were confident about their strength and their majority summed up with the emotional and political backing they received from the British. For them, 'Pakistan' could just be nothing except a dream eventually becoming a negligible part of history. But problems actually grew when this movement gained an unbelievably irresistible momentum and when it was clearly written in the eyes of every Indian Muslim that 'Pakistan was a reality'. Then the meaning of 'Pakistan' changed. Now, it was an insult for their 'majority and strength' when a materially 'weaker minority' was actually snatching a considerable part of their territory. But for them, still Pakistan was a temporary thing which, after the weaknesses they would gift it at the time of its birth, would soon collapse. However, Alhamdulillah, this meaning also never came into its actual being.

This was what Pakistan meant or was thought to mean at the time of its creation. Now I would try to show you the real picture of what 'Pakistan' means for us and for the rest of the world today!

For most of us, Pakistan is nothing except a country. In fact, a poor country with a corrupt leadership, unaware masses, growing international debts, pathetic living standards, terrorism, energy and food crisis, lack of the presence of basic human rights and hence each and every economic, social, political or religious problems ever thought by anyone prevail here in Pakistan. We do want to leave Pakistan because we do not consider it a country 'worthy to live in'. However, we are still not short of the people with contrasting ideas. They understand what Pakistan really 'means' and possess hearts filled to their deepest extent with a sincere patriotic attachment to Pakistan. They know the reason why Pakistan is something even 'worthy to be given the gift of one's life'. But let me give you a word of warning here. It is our nation which needs us, Pakistan or Islam are never in our need. In fact, we need Pakistan for our survival. Surely enough, nothing in the world can ever erase Pakistan or Islam and it should be an honor to be a part of the 'Pakistan' protected so dearly by the Creator of the Worlds. But if we continue this path of folly, maybe nature would be left with no choice other than replacing us with another nation more worthy of representing Islam and Pakistan. Be clear, Pakistan is not in danger, we are in danger! Therefore, we have to shift our ideas about the meaning of Pakistan as soon as possible to the second category of people described above. Remember, dear friends! Pakistan is a blessing, so give it the respect it deserves.

We would, now come to the enemy point of view about the meaning of Pakistan. Today, the enemies of Islam have cunningly but successfully brought the Muslims nearly to the edge of doom. They are cleverly controlling the political and hence, all internal issues of nearly the whole Islamic world. But still, Muslims never came to this state because of their defeats. Rather, Muslims are in this state because they are asleep. Still today, the whole Western world is terrified to the greatest extent by the mere thought of the awakening of Muslims. This is because Iqbal says:

تو مسلماں ہو تو تقدیر ہے تدبیر تری   ماسویٰ اللہ کے لیے آگ ہے تکبیر تری

(Translation:

For all else but God, your Takbeer is blazing fire,

If you a truly Muslim are, your effort is your fate.)

So our effort is our fate dear friends: Beautiful. In this situation the enemy is trying hard to get rid of one after another Muslim country in their 'state of sleep'. But today, Pakistan is the only country possessing such innumerable natural and military benefits that its awakening and standing up can bring extremely disastrous results for our enemies. This is the reason that, for them, Pakistan is a 'threat'. The truth of this fact is unraveled by the panic all our enemy nations are in to get rid of us. They have tried every scheme on us and have plotted unmatched cunning traps for us but our existence despite all this is a slap to their dignity. They know that Pakistan is something else, something stronger and undefeatable by experimented conspiracies. Hence, their attacks are severer and more secret. Terrorism and all other crisis inculcated in our country are still falling far too short to erase us and this is now becoming an ever-prolonged scheme. However, now it is on us that how we make our enemies to add some more ground realities about Pakistan to the meaning they already have for it.

But this is not all! Pakistanis have not come to barely survive and to strive unbearably hard to make both ends meet. Rather, we have come to lead and now, we have to realize our responsibility of answering all the questioning eyes of our Muslim Ummah looking towards us for support. Although the survival of Pakistan is, in itself, an unbelievable miracle but it is time to recognize our responsibilities as the saviors of both Islam and Pakistan. Now I would come to the final meaning of Pakistan in the eyes of the Islamic world. We are, without any doubt, the first Islamic nuclear power and are a huge military power in the Islamic world. We are the country whom every Muslim nation looks upon whenever in time of crisis and it in an honor for us. However, the enemies are creating differences in the Muslim world also and attempts are being made to disfigure this dignifying meaning of Pakistan. Some Muslim nations now regard us the allies of the West (thanks to our 'great' leadership) and the terrorism (gift from the West) is also harming our reputation there. Now, we are the ones who would prove Pakistan to be, truly, the 'Fortress of Islam'. This is our responsibility to save our country and then the whole Islamic world from the clouds of anti-Muslim atrocity prevailing everywhere most importantly in Kashmir, Afghanistan, Iraq, Burma and more recently, in Palestine.There's no choice left. WE HAVE TO DO IT!!!

Chapter 10. Politics and Power

In our country, these two words have and extraordinarily strong inter-relationship as politics over here, is always understood and used as means of getting power! In the eyes of most of our people, politics is an indecent profession because its image has been badly devastated by our national 'politicians'. Corruption and indecency are the basic interpretations of the word 'politics' engraved in the minds of today's common Pakistanis. However, in my thinking, these people are also justified with their stance as all the havoc in their lives and their country is merely due to the dishonesty and insincerity of the so called 'political leaders'!

Anyhow, this chapter has a broader purpose and hence, before anything else, let us glance through historic facts about the fights for 'politics and power' in Pakistan.

Although Quaid had given a firm and perfect foundation in every aspect for the new nation he had so recently built. He knew that he was suffering from tuberculosis and had a very little time to work for his nation but it was his toil which made Pakistan survive even in deadly impossible situations. His diligence in that one year of governor-generalship gave Pakistan a complete financial, economical, industrial, military, educational and social footing.

Figure 41: The toil of our great Quaid made Pakistan survive its early crucial days

But unfortunately, what we could not do was to make conditions strict to keep the desire of 'power' away from 'politics' after his death. Hence eventually, the strive for power with politics as the ladder initiated and now we stand where we are with not even a wink of patriotism or sincerity leftover in our so-called 'democratic' governmental setup.

Since after Jinnah, all governments have just given us nothing except a new set of ruins. Let me explain this to you in further detail. A deeply-rooted conspiracy brought about the assassination of Liaqat Ali Khan on October 16, 1951 and then the real disruption started. The folly of Malik Ghulam Muhammad initiated the dependence of the country on US aid and he soon became the first one to dissolve the constituent assembly based merely on personal discontents. Then came Iskander Mirza with a constitution of 1956 but along with a divided government and grave mistakes of 'One Unit Scheme' infuriating the Bengalis and then the declaration of martial law. Martial law brought Ayub Khan whose dictatorship gave a forced constitution of 1962, the harmful Tashkent Agreement regarding the war with India and unbearable US loans. Then the over-confidence of Yahya Khan summed up with the self-centeredness of Zulfiqar Ali Bhutto snatched East Pakistan from us in 1971. Bhutto's government then brought another constitution in 1973 but his 5-year long amendment program could just do nothing considerably positive in any field of the country situation. Zia's rule hanged Bhutto, brought Afghan refugees and with them it brought innumerable social vices summed up with an extremely destructive Klashnikov culture. Benazir's eras gave us nothing but broken promises, accusations of power snatching, a corruption master named Zardari and no progress except a negligible betterment in the 'foreign relations'. Nawaz Sharif's cunningness tried to win over the hearts of the people by giving us nuclear recognition and a motorway but at the cost of an ever-increasing drug abuse, unstoppable inflation, non-payable loans, massive corruption, a judiciary condemning drama and finally, a humiliating Kargil War. Then Musharraf's secularism took out every bit of Islamic modesty from the society, made alcohol drinking common, snatched our precious daughter of the nation Aafia Siddique from us and gave us tragedies like the US-Afghan war and the Lal

Masjid Disaster. Then Zardari's democracy gave us a stumbling industry, a staggering economy, irresistible poverty, massive injustice, terrorism, energy and food crisis and every problem anyone can think of a country to be having. Right now, our very own PMLN is well into its third era of rule over the country and until now, we seem to have achieved absolutely nothing obviously except a few new roads in Lahore. Today they sit in their parliaments with questions about the justification of their rule being raised everyday!

So, this was a very brief description of the distinctive qualities of our 'leaders'. However, they all had much in common as well. Firstly, they were no patriots and did not have even a slight love for their homeland. Even if a little 'likeness' was hidden somewhere in their hearts, it was always inferior to the love they had for each and every worldly possession whether huge or tiny. A thirst for power, authority and rule ran in their veins as they worked and strived hard only for themselves. This had induced a great degree of self-centeredness in them combined with a sense of indifference to everyone and everything else. Moreover, they were all feudal lords 'born to rule'. Their desire was merely limitless wealth and limitless power which was so easy to achieve via the ladder of people's emotions in a country of foolish masses like us. Our rate of poverty always remained alarming and the extravagancy of our 'leaders' always remained astonishingly distinctive from any other country in the whole world. They all robbed our home, destroyed us and then established their luxurious palaces on the ruins of our honor, pride and self-respect. They all pleaded for international aids even after knowing the natural potential Pakistan was having. They always begged for loans selling away the honor of the whole nation but more sadly, the money 'begged' was also not used for any betterment of the nation. Instead, the money taken from other countries in the name of Pakistan was and is still being constantly used by the governments to buy palaces and industries abroad and to fill out their own Swiss accounts. Their greed is never cured and their pockets never filled and what more to say, they do not even feel degraded or ashamed while asking for money.

But do not be misguided! It is surely their *hard-earned* money. They all were the servants of America serving in Pakistan and receiving payment as a reward. So what is wrong with that? Being a master traitor is in itself a very laborious job and deserves a lot. But unfortunately, they actually sold out their faith, their conscience, their country, their people and above all, the endless pleasures and rewards of the Hereafter indeed at a very low price. Holy Quran says:

"Do not exchange Allah's covenant for a small price. What is with Allah is better for you, if you only knew. What you have runs out, but what is with Allah remains. We will reward those who are patient according to the best of their deeds." (Al-Nahl; Ayah: 95, 96)

The final destiny of such people has also been described clearly in the Holy Quran:

"Those who sell out Allah's covenant, and their vows, for a small price, will have no share in the Hereafter, and Allah will not speak to them, nor will He look at them on the Day of Resurrection, nor will He purify them. They will have a painful punishment." (Al-e-Imran; Ayah: 77)

However, they are said to be involved sometimes in the betterment of the nation as well. But keeping in view their overall record, these are mere slight, occasional slips from their original firm footing designed only to befool us and to buy our votes. Furthermore, they all were there to divide our country and they made us fight between ourselves and then leave the passage clear for them. They have also kept us indulged in a never-ending political instability keeping us far away from thinking about other more important problems and their solutions. In short, they deserve no credit at all for any betterment done in our country but are solely responsible for the dismantling of our national 'system'.

The politicians are, without any doubt, the 'culprits' but there are also people who share nearly the same contribution in bringing about the present situation and those people are us_ the Pakistani nation itself. Most of you would be surely surprised at this sudden change of side but this is the actual reality. Our own nation brought these hypocrites into power. We, ourselves, gave them the chance and the pathway to sit in the Parliament, President and Prime Minister Houses and then to sign the warrants of our own destruction. Our fathers and forefathers elected these 'leaders' themselves by giving away their undeniable but unnoticed power of vote. The reason is that the people of our nation have always had a narrow range of thoughts or interests. Some of them elected their regional feudal lords merely terrified by their 'feudalism' and completely unaware of the fact that they are never in need of the feudal lords but rather, the feudal lords themselves need the people for continuing their landlord-ship as well as well as their politics. Some other did this to free their relatives from judicial cases or to keep up their repute as the lifelong supporters of a particular political party. Some needed a permanent powerful backing against the 'Thanas' (local police stations) while the most pathetic ones gave way to a national destruction for a petty price of mostly few hundred rupees only. Keeping up family pride or the habit of letting oneself to flow in the conventional currents of the society also became other major reasons for the robbers to reach the status of our rulers. Therefore, the electors had equal share in what the elected ones brought forth for the nation.

However, another typical mentality of our Pakistanis that we, ourselves, elect a government and when the democratic government shows its actual level of deeds, the same people curse its lethal acts day and night without even missing a single chance to condemn the government. When this government is replaced by martial law, the people celebrate the moments of getting rid of a corrupt government but before their eyes are opened, another 'more corrupt' dictatorship has already taken over and the people start protesting once again to get rid of the new system. Then elections follow and people elect the same politicians again and then the strangest thing happens when these people say:

"The previous era was at least better"

And so, the passage for the previous party of robbers is cleared of every hindrance as they can now come again and rob the nation with an even greater vigor. Tragically enough, when these 'haters of corrupt politicians' are asked to join politics themselves, they say:

"We are simple common people, what do we have to do with politics?"

And then this declaration of indifference from politics then leaves this precious field merely for such corrupt people and hence, we always face a lack of honest and patriotic leadership.

However, this situation should never last long at any cost. We, being the upcoming generation would be the next ones to elect and to decide the ones to have the right to govern us. We would be soon responsible for distinguishing the ones worthy of this post. So my dear brothers and sisters! Do acquire a considerable political knowledge in such circumstances as it is a serious need for our youth to be politically aware and active nowadays. Our Quaid said:

"You must concentrate on gaining knowledge. It is your foremost responsibility. Political awareness of the era is also part of your education. You must be aware of international events and environments. Education is a matter of life and death for our nation."

However, this never means that you should be exploited by any political party or to be misguided or misused by anyone. Your own political awareness should be strong enough for you to choose the right person worthy of your vote yourself. Quaid also said:

"You will be making the greatest mistake if you allow yourselves to be exploited by one political party or the other."

I have now made everything crystal clear to you including each and every quality of our previous rulers and also the mistakes of our earlier generations. Importance of political awareness has also been explained. Now the decision is open to you! Just remember one thing. Although we should believe that Allah is the obvious Sustainer and the

One Responsible for justice based accountability but He had Himself said in the Holy Quran:

"God does not change the condition of a nation until they change what is within themselves. And if God wills any hardship for a people, there is no turning back; and apart from Him they have no protector." (Al-Ra'ad; Ayah: 11)

Therefore, practical steps are also needed along with prayers to change our nation's political situation.

Dear friends! Vote is our authority and every authority given to people, whether on a large or small level, is a sacred trust by Almighty. If we waste it or more tragically, use it for someone like the previous rulers, we would stand answerable for the usage of our authority.

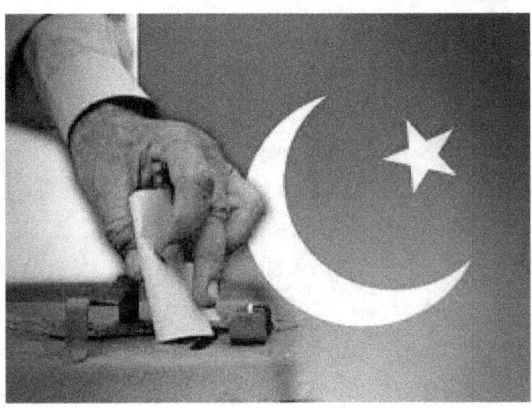

Figure 42: Your vote can bring a massive change, so never MISUSE or WASTE your chance to save Pakistan

Do take it as an advice from a Pakistani sister and please widen your interests to a national level while deciding where to vote for. Just because, Pakistan has surely had enough of the folly of its people and the dishonesties of its leaders!

Chapter 11. Foes Within and Without.

Friends and foes are an integral part and parcel of life for everyone. This same law applies to nations as well as it does on individual human beings. Nations also have friends and foes but a nation like us is bound to have such an insolvable mesh of friends and foes. As the upcoming youth of Pakistan, it is soon going to be our responsibility to correctly identify the 'foes' from amongst the 'friends' in both external and more importantly, the internal categories!

Hence, I would firstly like to discuss the more understandable topic which is 'foes without'. The external enemies of Pakistan can be easily identified by anyone of us as awareness in this aspect is common. But sadly enough, the depths of these enmities are not known by most of us and hence unknowingly, we actually become the ones to strengthen their conspiracies and play a vital role in our national devastation. At the top of this list lies our malicious eastern neighbor with all its bitter schemes designed to destroy us. Their enmity towards us is the obvious result of the feelings of vengeance because the areas now belonging to Pakistan once used to be a part of their 'Hindustan'. Our forefathers overcame their Hindu majority as well as their British support and cut open the chest of Hindustan to take out OUR PAKISTAN! Our existence is an insult for them and their jealousy is initiated from this fact. Although our survival as a nation proves the failure of their plots but as time passes these plots become severer and more cunning.....

In order to weaken our agriculture, they break the Indus Water Treaty every year blocking the water of the Chenab River in water shortage days and opening it up again in monsoons becoming the ones to initiate floods in the lowland areas of Punjab and Sindh. Then to make our economy stagger and to hurt our reputation in the world, our impression as a 'terrorist' nation is spread overwhelmingly. Moreover, they also provide a lot of funds to supply financial help to the 'international' band of terrorists working in Pakistan. Their spies also work day and night trying hard to find and bribe traitors from the nation. Their media is also never left behind in teasing us and showing a false picture of Muslims and of Pakistan to a humiliating extent. They have occupied Kashmir and are carrying out an unstopped and continuous massacre of innocent Muslims and they have fought four wars with us as well. They also developed nuclear weapons for us, formed friendly relations with Russia and now with America to handle us. They are just willing to do anything to get rid of Pakistan....

Figure 43: Traditional rivals

But we, being the Pakistani youth, are the real treasure of this nation and unfortunately, they are out to destroy us as well. I was personally brought to tears when I heard an Indian politician saying on television:

"The youth of Pakistan can do nothing against us. Our media alone is enough to tackle with them."

But their media is actually doing whatever the politician said. So my dear brothers and sisters! Are we still stupid enough to become a vital role player in this open scheme? It has been planned accurately to make our active, precious, working age useless for Pakistan. We obviously do this for entertainment purpose, but this so called 'entertainment' is left far behind when the young ones actually try and start practicing what they see on cinema and television screens. But it is our apparent bad luck that we, although being far better than our neighbor country's youth in all aspects, still try to copy their mode of living hence degrading our social and ethical values ourselves which are our precious discrimination. We are asleep. Asleep to the extent that the enemy can even dare to announce what it has planned and still there is not even the slightest change in our behavior. Wake up! We have already had enough of them. Although we know that we lost East Pakistan in 1971 not because of their supremacy but because of our own mistakes, but still we have got to seek revenge now! Of everything they did in 1947, in 1971 and are still doing in Kashmir. And this revenge is going to be sought by throwing their schemes back at their ugly faces. It is going to be sought by becoming better Muslims and patriotic Pakistanis and by proving that they've failed in converting us into what they wanted.

However India's jealousy is limited to Pakistan because they only have the hysterical wish of getting 'their land' back. But our more dangerous enemies are other powers. To start with, I would firstly like to share an ayah of Surah Baqarah of the Holy Quran:

"The Jews and Christians will not approve of you, unless you follow their creed. Say, "God's guidance is the guidance"......"(Al-Baqarah; Ayah: 120)

Here, the Quran has already told us 1460 years ago that Jews and Christians can never be our friends unless we follow what they say. So aren"t we following whatever America and Israel are dictating? I know that the minds of most of you people would have definitely thought about our government....... But no! I am not talking about the government. Rather, I am talking about us! Leave all that government and leadership on one side. Leave everything else...... Leave the selling of country interests for American dollars. Leave the enslavement of our government in front of America and Israel, leave the devastation of our country due to their direct involvement in our issues and leave the lack of concern of our leaders for Palestinian Muslims. Just leave everything else and think about you yourself! Aren't 'we' slaves to American culture and Israeli industrial products? Isn't it present in our national instinct that a feeling of honor is aroused in our hearts whenever we happen to talk to or even see anyone belonging to those countries? Isn't America a dreamland for most of our youth? Aren't their people our role models? Ask these questions from yourself and re read the verse above….. Yes! We do follow what they say even when we know that they are not and can never be our friends.

We do try our fullest to act, eat, drink and live like them. This enslavement is on every level but the most dangerous part is us, the youth. Have we forgotten that we are the guardians of the Holy Ka'aba, the guardians of Holy Quran and now the guardians of Pakistan? Don't we know that our social values are a treasure for us and we are throwing this treasure away in the ocean with our own hands? We can be far better on individual level from those people, so why do we follow them? We have ourselves lowered our status in the world and have forgotten the real purpose of our lives!

And we have forgotten something else as well. We have forgotten how our Muslim brothers have died and are still dying mainly in Palestine, Iraq and Afghanistan. We have forgotten to respond to the wailing cries of thousands of daughters of Islam who are dishonored every day by our barbarian *role models* in Palestine, Iraq and Afghanistan. The unimaginable but 100% real atrocities are forgotten. The Israeli election policy has always been a massacre of Palestinian Muslims but we just don't know. Muslim blood is flowing everywhere and we are actually trying to be inspired by the nations responsible for this mass annihilation of Muslim culture and identity. They are the real enemies of Islam and because Pakistan was, is, and shall always be an important Islamic country, so they are the enemies of Pakistan too. But no! Our *developed* culture seems to be too important for us to ignore it. We just cannot prefer the all significant education over the addicting involvements mainly facebook and mobiles designed so perfectly for us. We cannot restrict ourselves to our cultural and moral values because their culture is modern and this so called 'modernization' is so essential for development! But can any 'modernized' brother tell me that how is it possible that a Muslim daughter of Pakistan (Dr. Aafia Siddique) is tortured to an unimaginable extent when at the same time; millions of her Muslim Pakistani brothers lay asleep in their cozy beds? But we did it and are still doing it for most of us are unaware of the consequences. So get yourself ready to hear the result of this behavior and…….. Read the full ayah:

"The Jews and Christians will not approve of you, unless you follow their creed. Say: "God's guidance is the guidance". Should you follow their desire after the knowledge has come to you, you will have in Allah neither Guardian nor Helper." (Al-Baqarah; Ayah: 120)

I hope all of you are sensible enough to understand the word of warning given to us in this ayah. But we need our Allah, our Guardian, and our Helper! Without Him or His Help, we'll be destroyed in both the worlds. For God's sake stop following those devils blindly! They kill your brothers, they dishonor your sisters and mothers in the light of the day, they call you terrorists, and they even dare to insult your Prophet (PBUH) and his teachings. What else is left to be done which would finally awaken you from this fatal sleep? It is fine if you don't believe me. If it still seems right to you, keep up your actions but nevertheless, you have to believe in the Holy Quran and then, according to Quran, you would never find Allah as a Guardian or Helper of your nation!

This was what could have been said to warn you of external dangers. But more serious and dangerous are the internal ones who would be discussed here as 'foes within' which are extremely difficult to recognize. This aspect includes the 'terrorist' group as the foremost member. Although we think that we can recognize them easily but remember, that even under the name 'terrorists', their lies a mesh of friends and foes! Let me solve it for you.

Americans and Israeli troops kill innocent civilian Muslims anywhere they want with the worst scenarios of inhumane brutalities but they are as innocent in the eyes of the world as they can ever be. On the other hand, Pakistan has sacrificed more than 35000 of its troops and civilians and has emptied its economy in the name of this 'war on terror' and still the world calls Pakistan the real terrorist country. However, as a quotation goes on saying:

"The situation when you are right but the world thinks you are wrong is far better than the situation when you are wrong but the world thinks you are right."

So, it is apparently not the world which matters. What matters in deciding the right and wrong is your own inner self! Uphold this situation and feel proud and contented to be on the right side. The practical steps towards betterment only come after this feeling. Here, another piece of advice is very essential. Never ever degrade your identity by trying to hide it when you are abroad, just in order to save yourselves from the tag of belonging to a terrorist nation. Rather, rise up and tell it from your actions that you are a proud, sincere Pakistani Muslim and not a terrorist.

Secondly, you should be told that there used to be an Afghan band of Mujahidin earlier on who were trained officially by Pakistan and were backed and aided by the USA only to fight against the Russians. But then the drama of the crashing of world tower was done and then cunningly, the innocuous, nearly poor and local Tehrik-e-Taliban was entangled deliberately with the international Al-Qaeda and was hence accused of equal interference. As a result, Afghanistan was captured which was illegal from every context of world rules. In reality, those Taliban Mujahidin were not terrorists or even extremists. Rather, they were just fundamentalist Muslims who always legally fought only against the invader forces, either America or Russia. Then, to indulge the strong neighbor Pakistan also got involved in an 'imposed' war, a fake Tehrik-e-Taliban was formed which consisted of 'extremist non-Muslims' and this band of enemies of Islam and Pakistan was poured into Pakistan. I am forced to say all this because it was revealed during the recent military operation that much of the masterminds of the terrorist industry were always found to be non-Muslims and non-Pakistanis. However, the brainwashed children who are kept ahead are always children of innocent Pakistani Muslims. Another point to prove this that this Tehrik-e-Taliban of Pakistan has no link with the real Tehrik-e-Taliban is that these Taliban are carrying out a scheme which is extremely costly in terms of finances and arms while a local party of an already occupied country can never fulfill the supply. Their actual supply comes from America, India and Israel who are united together in trying out this scheme to harm Pakistan. Yet another proof of the real terrorists being non-Muslims is that they always hit a mosque or a public gathering and we know that these targets do not harm Islam. However, they never attack bars, pubs or clubs which are always meant to harm the 'Islam' of this society. On the other hand, the real Afghan Taliban are still fighting to their last breath against the invader NATO forces who have unjustly occupied their motherland. The fact that these real Taliban are nearly short of resources is clearly reflected from the less quantity and less destructiveness of the attacks they are able to make on the NATO forces.

Then, as the next part of this plot, American drones illegally fly over the Pakistani borders whenever they want to and kill innocent tribal people of Northern Pakistan claiming wrongly to kill terrorists from amongst the 'Pakistani tribes of Waziristan'.

Figure 44: American drones are not even questioned for violating the sovereignty of Pakistan whenever they want!

These drones are a crystal clear proof of the status of our politicians sitting in any kind of government as they never speak against drones telling us that they have no concern with the sovereignty of Pakistan. But do not be misled. Our air-force is never weak or unable to detect or hit these drones. Rather, they have to await any such orders from our civilian ruling elite. These drones just do nothing except increasing the number of terrorists for Pakistan. This is done easily by creating a large group of those people whose dear ones are killed in the drones and the justly rebellious minds of these people are then exploited to make them perfect terrorists to damage Pakistan.... So I hope that most of the knots in your minds concerning this topic would have been eased and now you would be more able to at least 'recognize' the real terrorists who are never Muslims!

Then there is your second internal enemy, which is the existing conventional system of our society. This system hinders the actual democracy (not at all the type advocated by the PPP and the PMLN) and the lack of democracy stops us from being what we potentially can be. This system of feudalism, 'Thana' culture, government controlled judicial and legal system, bribery and corruption at every level_ this system is our enemy and we have to fight against it and defeat it at any cost. But many of us are, rather unknowingly, becoming a part of this system almost every day. We can never develop if we ever become like the people who cannot produce enough courage to stand up, even alone, against this system. Rather, such people just accept that it cannot be changed and instead of trying, they absorb in the system making it worse. These 'followers of conventional system' break country laws deliberately and then say with a relaxed heart:

"Oh don't worry! It's Pakistan. Anything can be done over here."

This pathetic mindset of our people needs to be changed by us, through denying this system and rising against it even when everyone mocks at us. Moreover, this system is of hopelessness and we would have to fight against hopelessness at every step we would take against the system. But we have to make ourselves strong to change the system the way which leads to our boost and our development as enough harm has been already done by it.

Furthermore, never to omit, we also have other internal enemies in the form of corrupt feudal politicians whose purposes are narrowed to their individual beings and they devastate the country. Moreover, anyone or even anything which tends to disunite or break our nation or whatever tries to cover us with the dark clouds of hopelessness or increases our sluggishness or jumbles up our friends and foes is absolutely our internal enemy. But my friends, a country like ours is bound to be having so many malicious enemies so never be afraid, but just beware!

Chapter 12. Defenders of The Holy Land

Life is the most precious worldly possession anyone can claim to have and hence, sacrificing this dearest life for someone becomes the apex of all acts designed to prove love. But when this life is sacrificed for Allah, for His Islam and for His Muslims, this act becomes the apex of all honors anyone can ever dream to have. Adopting a profession which ultimately leads to this sacrifice is in itself the noblest act and so, this part of my book is dedicated to this profession, and to our defenders, the fabulous PAKISTAN ARMY!

The Pakistani nation has always looked upon its army as the most disciplined and honored profession in both worldly and religious aspects and so its reputation in the world is unquestioned. But who would believe that all this started with the most negligible resources! Let me tell you this in the form of an interesting comparison......

The Pakistan Armed Forces had to start their journey in the most vulnerable conditions ever seen by history. The armed forces and military equipment was to be divided between Pakistan and India in the ratio of 5:17 according to the respective populations. However, tragically, Pakistan was not even given 1% of its shares and even the equipments Pakistan received after so many delays were always worn-out, damaged and unusable ordnance stores and military vehicles. These supplies also arrived late and the officer allotted to fulfill the job of this division of military assets resigned even before his job was completed. Furthermore, Pakistan was not even given one out of the former 16 ordnance factories in India so that it could at least start producing its own weapons to defend itself. The early defenders of our land did not even have highly ranked officers to train them and hence, Quaid had to borrow 500 British officers to train his army temporarily.

Figure 45: The PAK army in its early days with Quaid in the background

An army, facing such doldrums along with an eternal enemy neighbor many times stronger than itself in military respect, was bound to perish. But it survived. And not only survived, it flourished to become one of the best trained armies of the whole world competing with the super powers in terms of training and defending every inch of the holy land....

Can anyone of you tell me what was there with our army when materially nothing was there? What is still there with them which empower's them to sacrifice their everything for Pakistan? What enables them to live in extreme climatic conditions in the greatest mountain ranges of the whole world and still fight against an enemy three times larger than them both in terms of quantity and weapons? The answer to all these questions lies in their spiritual strength, their faith in Allah, their belief in His help, their inner satisfaction for doing the most meritorious act and above all, it is their desire for martyrdom which has always been their real weapon. Obviously, defeating an army in which every single person has the greatest desire to die for his country and his religion is not at all an easy task and this was soon revealed when the world saw the Pakistan army in action immediately after independence. So my dear brothers and sisters! Read this brief historic account and then rationally decide about your future thoughts concerning your army.

The Indians had attacked so early in October 1947, but still it was our seriously under-resourced and weaponless army which completely stopped them from accomplishing their dirty task of entering Pakistan through the pathway of Kashmir. But it was not all, the same army had also actually driven away the Indian cowards out of Kashmir when their government had to run away and cry for help in the UN. What followed was the ceasefire but Pakistan only agreed to withdraw its forces from Kashmir warning India that it had to hold an honest plebiscite in Kashmir for the Kashmiri people to decide the country they opted to join. But then again, as the deceitful nature of Hindus can never be changed, so they broke this one of their promises as well and not surprisingly, no plebiscite has been held up-to-date. The UN also took no notice of this deceit as it is also over-whelmed by the enemies of Islam and Pakistan. Then in 1965, Pakistani military and Para-military forces crossed the line of control (LOC), entered and attacked the Indian-occupied Kashmir after being provoked by India and had even besieged the cowards of Indian Army inside Kashmir. India, hence, retaliated and attacked Lahore and Sialkot simultaneously from land and air. They were thinking that they could easily gain these border cities as all the Pakistan army was busy fighting in Kashmir. But then our brave soldiers made history and defended these strategic cities unbelievably. The Indian army officials had even formally announced that they would celebrate the next evening in the streets of Lahore but our warriors did not even allow them to touch the official boundaries of Lahore. Then the sky saw single Pakistani military companies overcoming whole of the coward Indian battalions near Lahore. Then four seemingly antique aircrafts of the PAF were seen destroying 25 fully modern and deadly fighter jets of the Indian Air Force simultaneously destroying the Anbala Airbase. Then a handful of Pakistani soldiers were seen forcing 600 enemy tanks to retreat and run away and then 5 enemy aircrafts were destroyed by a single (even less technologically advanced) aircraft controlled by Sir M.M.Alam in 1 minute creating an unbelievable world record. This seems unrealistic but it was done by our pride, our army. Then in 1971, India illegally plunged into our own personal matters and started training a rebel force named 'Mukti Bahini' and then declared war. But it was never their superiority; but instead, it was the betrayal of our own Bengali brothers and the mistakes of our rulers which snatched East Pakistan from us. Then it was our army which captured Kargil and India had to run away to the UN again.

Figure 46: The Defenders of the Holy Land

In short, it has always been exactly the case what Noor Jahan says here:

(Translation:

Those who came to burn away the abode,

Verily, your blood extinguished those flames;

For you have saved from orphanage many flowers,

And have preserved the fragrances of numerous springs.

The breezes of the garden salute thee.

O martyrs for the right cause! O embodiments of sincerity!

The winds of the motherland salute thee.)

Now that you have read the account, let me tell you the reason for including this chapter in a book meant for the Pakistani youth. It lies in the fact that time and enemy plots have obscured the reputation of this strongest institution of our country as well and now a great number of our youth seems to be fed up and dismayed from our own army. This is seriously tragic, but more importantly, this can be destructive for our army and consequently, for our nation as well. Isn't it true that most of us think that like all other professions, army is also giving away to corruption now? Although such people have no proof for their accusations but they always end up saying that the army once used to be an admirable profession but its majority is corrupt and only a minority leftover is patriotic in the true terms! But I just have one question for them all. Can anyone of them just step out of their homes when they know that their country is in danger and their own life is at stake? The answer, simply, is no! Because to step out to save the honor of your country and of Islam when you know that an obvious death awaits you needs an incredible amount of self-control, dauntless devotion for Islam and Pakistan and an unshaken courage which has always been the all-important legacy of the Armed Forces of Pakistan. In an answer to all such blames on my army, I would just say it rationally that it is only our army and defense system due to which we have survived four deadly wars and are still breathing in an independent air. But it is true that we have forgotten many things we should have remembered as a nation. Every inch of the boundary line has incredible stories of untold braveries and unmatched courage. Yes! Every inch has been irrigated by the sacred blood of those people who have always defended the holy land in a way no other could do.

In short, we cannot find even a single expression of such valor or patriotism in the recent past which could stand parallel to the fearlessness summed up with faith in Allah which enabled Rashid Minhas Shaheed to crash his own plane to protect Pakistani military secrets from reaching India, which empowered Major Raja Aziz Bhatti Shaheed to defend the whole Lahore with a single battalion and to stand fearlessly upright in front of dozens of enemy tanks, which motivated Captain Muhammad Sarwar Shaheed to move ahead and cut the barbed wire amongst automatic firing, which encouraged Major Tufail Muhammad Shaheed to drive out a much larger Indian attacking 'coward' company, which stimulated Jawan Sawar Muhammad Hussain Shaheed to fight and destroy 16 enemy tanks merely with a few people, which helped Major Muhammad Akram Shaheed to repulse every land and air attack from a many times larger and stronger enemy in the front area, which induced an inborn fearlessness in Lance Naik Muhammad Mahfuz Shaheed making him enter and enemy bunker alone, injured and unarmed to strangle an enemy soldier controlling the machine gun to death, which convinced Major Shabbir Sharif Shaheed to hold down three enemy battalions with a single company, which allowed Captain Karnal Sher Khan Shaheed to hold and defend five strategic posts with one company even in extreme conditions, which persuaded Havaldar Lalak Jan Shaheed to volunteer for being deployed on the front line and which allows each and every soldier of the Pakistan Army till today to sacrifice everything he has only for the 'dear motherland'.

Figure 47: The Nishan-e-Haider, Highest military award of Pakistan (left), the Nishan-e-Haider holders (right)

Iqbal said:

یہ غازی، یہ تیرے پُراسرار بندے
جنہیں تُو نے بخشا ہے ذوقِ خدائی

دو نیم ان کی ٹھوکر سے صحرا و دریا
سمٹ کر پہاڑ ان کی ہیبت سے رائی

دو عالم سے کرتی ہے بیگانہ دل کو
عجب چیز ہے لذتِ آشنائی

شہادت ہے مطلوب و مقصودِ مومن
نہ مالِ غنیمت نہ کشورکشائی

(Translation:

These warriors, victorious, these mysterious worshippers of Yours,

Whom you have granted the will to win Power in Your Name;

Who cleave woods and rivers in twain.

Whose terror turns mountains into dust, O Lord!

It dismays the heart from the pleasures of this world,

Strange is the feeling of acknowledgement;

The purpose and sole aim of a true believer is martyrdom,

Not the rule of the earth, nor the war booty; O Lord!)

But my dear brothers and sisters! In response to all these continuous sacrifices, can we not even respect the ones laying their lives for our freedom? Can we just imagine that every night if we sleep peacefully, it is just because our soldiers are awake at the borders? We have to change this thought and stop ourselves from falling prey to yet another conspiracy from our enemies. Our army is obviously the only thing which stops them from seizing our country and we have to own it and uphold it to the highest degree of esteem.

Now, concerning the accusations about corruption, Iqbal had already said:

آئیں جوامراں حق گوئی و بے باکی   اللہ کے شیروں کو آتی نہیں روباہی

(*Translation:*

Men bold and firm uphold the truth and let no fear assail their hearts,

No doubt, the mighty Lions of Allah know no tricks, know no arts.)

However, saying that the army is not corrupt never means that everyone in this profession is an angel. There are obviously, traitors in the robes of nobility but due to such people, degrading the whole army is, by all means, a folly! I do not mean to say that every act carried out so far by any one belonging to the army is legal. For verily, it was the army which gave birth to dictators like Ayub Khan, Yahya Khan, Zia-ul-Haq and Musharraf. Yes it was the same army which surrendered in Dhaka and it was still the same army which killed hundreds of innocent children in Lal Masjid. But mind you, it was the army leadership which mattered in all these cases. But whatever was there, the army surely held a highly prestigious stature for the whole nation before Musharraf's era.

Figure 51: General Pervaiz Musharraf

It can be surely remembered as the darkest era in the history of Pakistan military. It was Musharraf who even encouraged alcohol drinking amongst Muslim Pakistani soldiers. It was him who ordered the Lal Masjid disaster and under him, the army and the police handed over the daughter of the nation, Aafia Siddique to America. It was still Musharraf under whom, the army actually aided America in raiding a Muslim neighbor country. It was him who undermined the whole army and whose era made people think that like everything else, the army too had changed.

But this can not last any longer. The real culprit has been the leadership while still today, each and every soldier, even of the lowest rank has the same purpose; sacrificing their lives for Pakistan. If not anything else, we would have to respect our army at least at this basis that they die for our lives. But this is never the real status they deserve. In reality, their status is unimaginable and never comprehendible by the minds of common people like us. The Prophet (PBUH) had said:

"The warrior in the path of Allah is equal to the man who observes fasting regularly, stands before Allah in worship and recites the verses of Allah, not resting from tiredness through fasting and worship."

The Holy Quran also describes the greatness of such people in the following words:

"Those who believe, and suffer exile and strive with might and main, in Allah's cause, with their goods and their persons, have the highest rank in the sight of Allah...." (Al-Taubah; Ayah: 20)

Other innumerable ayahs of the Holy Quran describe the reward for fighters in the cause of Allah.

Then it is 'martyrdom', the greatest rank any Muslim can ever dream to reach. It is the choicest blessing of Almighty for which He only chooses the best of His people. Because of this rank of our 'Defenders of the Holy Land', all other mistakes fall far too short in front of the martyrdom which they seek in their job. Holy Quran says:

"..... To him who fights in the cause of Allah_ whether he is slain or gets victory_ soon shall we give him a reward of great (value)." (Al-Nisa; Ayah: 74)

Holy Quran also says elsewhere:

"And say not of those who are slain in the way of Allah, 'they are dead'. Nay they live, finding their sustenance in the presence of their Lord." (Al-e-Imran; Ayah: 169)

So my dear brothers and sisters! Where else can we find such defenders of our freedom? Who else has such courage and patriotism for Pakistan other than our armed forces? Who else can sacrifice everything that he has only for the honor of Islam and Pakistan and for repaying the 'debt of the motherland'? Surely, no one else other than our soldiers. They are our pride and we would have to respect them to the utmost limit giving them the status they deserve both in worldly and religious aspects.

Chapter 13. Can We Save Pakistan?

It has been explained to you with many essential details that Pakistan was formed under unimaginably poor conditions. Its ever-lasting enemy, aided by the British had cunningly eradicated everything on which the newly born country could rely for its survival. Pakistan never got even half of its share in the industries and financial assets of the former India. Pakistan had no cities developed considerably by the British. At the time of creation, the government was so poor that it could hardly manage the salary of its officials merely for one single month. The government officials did not have money to buy even pens and paper to carry out the office work. There were few or no experienced Muslim statespersons, government officials, businessmen, industrialists, management experts or economists. The country did not have a single bank, airline or any developed sea post. All of the most agriculturally fertile lands had been given to India and to deprive the Pakistani Punjab of most of its waters as well, all head-works for the rivers and canals flowing in Pakistan were now located in Indian controlled Punjab.

So, Pakistan was just left with nothing India could be feared of, while doing anything it wanted. Then, an influx of millions of homeless, penniless and panic-stricken people into a country already surrounded by crisis was also made inevitable. To provoke Pakistan further, Indian annexation of Junagadh, Hyderabad (Deccan) and then of Kashmir was enough to mobilize its seriously under-resourced army into a war. After knowing all this, it is not difficult to understand that our country was vulnerable and seriously exposed to dangers from all sides. Who could say that it could survive even a few months? In fact the Indian political leaders and thinkers from all over the globe were firmly convinced that within a year, Jinnah would realize, retaliate and then 'beg' for a reunion. But the whole world was proved wrong...

But these were the doldrums of 1947 only. Even after this initial phase, which crisis, problem or disaster ever occurred on the surface of Earth has not been faced by Pakistan? It is still facing innumerable problems and we are fully aware of them. But even today, can anyone rationally predict a survival after such problems? But Pakistan survived, and is still surviving each and every upheaval. However, nothing in this world is ever without a reason. So there are, by all means, solid reasons behind the ability of our country to come out unbelievably from impossible problems even when our status as a nation is not worthy of surviving. Dear brothers and sisters! Here I would like to reflect upon some of these important reasons.

Firstly and most importantly, our country was the first and is the only country which was fought and achieved merely on religious lines with its foundations laid in the name of Allah. The common slogan raised by every freedom fighter in 1947 was no other than:

What is the meaning of Pakistan?

There is no God but Allah.

Pakistan was an unbelievable miracle for the whole world but for Muslims, this miracle was a gift granted by Almighty on the 27th of Ramadan. It was a response from the Merciful Lord to all of the sacrifices those calamity-stricken people had made. Hence, they are surely the unseen powers of nature which have guarded Pakistan so far miraculously in all doldrums. It is Allah who is protecting the piece of land which was separated and the country which was founded in His Holy Name. Although there are other reasons also, but even if there was no other reason to assist the fact that it was made in Allah's name, Pakistan would still have survived. But nevertheless, it is truly a fact that all other reasons seem utterly subservient to this one cause. Just because it was Allah Who wanted to save Pakistan and hence He created co-incidents and assisting factors to help Pakistan survive!

Figure 52: The country created in His Holy name can never be destroyed

However, as we are here to discuss everything so I would surely tell you about a few other important reasons as well. The second reason is that the land allotted in 1947 to Pakistan has always been irrigated continuously with the blood of innumerable martyrs. To me, Pakistan survived also because it was born to survive because nature had started its preparations centuries ago when Muhammad bin Qasim entered Sindh for the very first time. Islam was then introduced with its full glory in the form of the mercy, sympathy and unbelievably kind behavior of Muhammad bin Qasim. This was done in a land of infidels only because later on, this Islam was going to become the basis of all struggle for Pakistan. This was also the first supply of martyr blood to this land which was dying to hear the thumping of horses' hooves owned by Muslim warriors. Then after some time, Mahmud Ghaznavi was sent by nature to shake out the 'mandirs' of Hindustan and to revive Islam, with his soldiers further increasing the number of brave martyrs who died in this region. Then Sultan Muhammad Ghauri, Qutub-uddin Aibak followed by the slave dynasty, Delhi Sultanate and then finally, the Mughals were all steps towards Pakistan and a further increase in the sacred martyr blood irrigating the land of Pakistan. Then in 1947, in both the wings of Pakistan, Muslims were slaughtered ruthlessly everywhere and it seems as if even the boundaries were drawn by the blood of innocent martyrs. Moreover, since 1947, millions of martyrs of Pakistan Army have protected every inch of the motherland. Therefore, all the souls of these holy martyrs are another strong support for Pakistan against every difficulty.

By now, you all would have guessed another unforgettably important factor helping Pakistan to survive. And this was, undoubtedly, the unshaken leadership of the Father of the Nation, Quaid-e-Azam Muhammad Ali Jinnah. His determination was one of the greatest causes for the formation of Pakistan and henceforth, his toil was letting Pakistan to survive its initial crucial days. Such a new country as Pakistan badly needed a perfect, honest leader and nature gifted it in the form of Quaid. He knew that he had made Pakistan after an enormous struggle only for the reason that it should survive till the Day of Judgment. He also knew all the crises his country was facing along with all the 'realistic' predictions which were being made worldwide about Pakistan. But he also knew that he had very little time to work for the country he had fought so hard to get, as he knew he was suffering from tuberculosis. But he wasted exactly none of that 'little time' and worked tirelessly fulfilling the duties of many posts at the same time and trying laboriously to stabilize the country and the nation.

Figure 53: Our Great Quaid

He founded a government, an economy, a national security and most importantly, he founded a nation. As Professor Stanley Wolpert says in his book 'Jinnah of Pakistan':

"Few individuals significantly alter the course of history. Fewer still modify the map of the world. Hardly anyone can be credited with creating a nation. Muhammad Ali Jinnah did all three."

These were some of the reasons why Pakistan survived in its early days when no one could even think of it doing so. But miracles are not new to our history, both as Muslims, and as Pakistanis as well. However, if we analyze today's situation, we would find each and every 'mature' Pakistani and everyone who is aware of the circumstances in Pakistan only saying:

"Pakistan has no solution."

But my dear brothers and sisters, I do assure you that Pakistan has solutions. These problems can never ever harm our country to the extent of destroying it. Rather, these are merely a test. Iqbal said:

تو سمجھتا ہے یہ ساماں ہے دل آزاری کا،‏ خود داری کا امتحاں ہے ترے ایثار کا

(Translation:

You deem this a cause of grief; your heart is mortified,

But no your pride, your sacrifice, thus, once again, are tried.)

Furthermore, nature has already gifted us everything but we only lack a proper usage of them. Revolutions do occur so why are we so hopeless about revolutions concerning Pakistan? Although it is true that Pakistan today is standing at the edge of endless destruction but there surely is always a way back:

نہ چو نومید، نومیدی زوال علم و عرفاں ہے

امیدِ مردِ مومن ہے خدا کے رازدانوں میں

(Translation:

Despair not, for despair is the decline of knowledge and gnosis,

The hope of a Believer is among the confidents of God.)

So don't despair dear Pakistanis; for our hope is 'among the confidents of God'.

We, surely, are a nation divided into every possible religious or regional sects any one can think of. We do encounter a tantalizing terrorism which has eaten up our economy along with our reputation and is now busy eating up our army. We do face a humiliating power and energy crisis. There is surely water shortage in our country. Our imports have always exceeded the quota of our exports. Our industries are rapidly closing down increasing the already massive unemployment. It is obviously us who are graduated and fabulously talented but young people like us are forced to work as laborers in order to earn a living, while the most unfortunate ones end up becoming a part of the ever increasing drug abuse or sometimes they become nothing except angry, revengeful criminals. It is our society where moral and social values have been suffocated to death in the humidity of secularism and liberalism. It is our nation who's sensational or sympathetic feelings for anyone have been squeezed till the last drop. It is our nation who blindly runs after western culture and modes of living. We are the nation to invent new heinous crimes and have no practically enforced law to stop us from doing that. We are the ones with all our useful brains being drained out. We are the people who bring forth the worst apathetic tyrants ever known to history. We, ourselves, accept the leaders who devastate us and when the next band of even worse leaders comes to power, we start praising the last ones just because we are the most stupid group of people on the surface of earth. We are the Islamic Republic whose precious daughter is being abducted day and night and we just do nothing. We are the powerless, sluggish people who cannot even get rid of a government destroying us in the light of the day. Yes! We are strangled by feudalism from all aspects and many of us even seem to accept it. Our peace keeping and law enforcement forces are known to the whole world for their 'honest' services. No doubt, we are littered with every kind of corruption from the top to the bottom. We are the incredible nation who has been burdened by an unbearable weight of foreign loans when an unimaginable amount of Pakistani investments are resting in the Swiss Banks. We are the country whose enemies are intervening and 'controlling' us with the most cunning ease. Yes! We are the exterminated nation of Pakistan whose long survival is the most 'unrealistic' joke of today!

But wait! Isn't it us who still have the capability of keeping the lamp alight amidst every storm? Even if we seem to be divided into sects, isn't it our nation which becomes an example of unity whenever calamity strikes? Even if we do face terrorism and our reputation has been badly affected but isn't it our nation who is fighting and clearly winning against the terrorism which is clearly aided by the 'super powers' of the world? Even if we have a power and energy crisis, don't we possess the resources to eliminate this? Although our economy is stumbling but aren't we having people capable of restoring it? Even if we have lost all behavior codes as a nation, don't we possess the ultimate guidance as the Holy Quran to guide us? Although we are growing insensate but aren't we still the nation which donates the most in the whole world? Even if we are the nation to produce dictators, isn't it the same nation to give birth to people like Abdul Sattar Edhi and brilliants like Arfa Kareem and Dr. Abdul Qadeer Khan? Although the government is unacceptable, but don't we have the right to vote and the time to think truly where to vote next in order to change the system? Even if the enemy is out to attack us at any time, but aren't we having the seventh largest army of the world, a nuclear power, a zealous nation and above all, the help of the Almighty to resist it? Yes we do! Although our nation is asleep and is also injured but it is not at all dead! We are the people winning fabulous laurels in every field we step into. Although the system is corrupt but we, the new generation, can remain free of corruption. <u>Yes, we can obviously save Pakistan Insha Allah</u>. It was the youth which played a key role in the formation of Pakistan and it is my belief that it is again going to be the youth which is destined to save Pakistan.

However, in order to achieve this goal, many paths can be followed but there is a condition for us to become a 'searcher' in order to accomplish any such task. Iqbal said:

کوئی قابل ہو تو ہم شانِ کئی دیتے ہیں

ڈھونڈنے والوں کو دنیا بھی نئی دیتے ہیں

(*Translation:*

On him who merits will I set the brightest diadem.

And those who truly questing come, a new world waits for them.)

Although our deeds and the circumstances surrounding us make us think that Allah is no more on our side but the matter is totally different for the country. No matter how sinful we become and likewise, no matter how difficult our lives become in this world, we can perish but Pakistan has to live till the morning of the Day of Resurrection. Although Allah can punish us whenever He wishes but this country was made in His name and He shall protect it Insha Allah by one way or the other. Because:

"The light of God looks upon the intrigues of the infidels,

This lamp can never be extinguished by mere blows of the breath."

Chapter 14. The Base of all Progress: Education

Education is, without any doubt, the sole discriminator between human beings and animals as knowledge and the curiosity to gain it are the only few qualities which differentiate us from all other living creatures. Education is truly the requirement to pour 'humanity' into a human and then blend it with an honorable, civilized mode of life....

However, these were the clear cut facts about education which we all know by heart. But what we do not know is the implication of these facts. Dear brothers and sisters! Do mind it that education has actually become equivalent to oxygen in terms of its significance for survival in this world. Everyone does need to be fully educated in order to be called human beings in the first place! The whole world is running frantically in the race for education, awareness and scientific technology and hence, anyone who even lowers his pace is instantly toppled over and trampled by this huge wild trampede. But whatever it is, it is the reality and we have no option other than accepting it and getting ourselves ready for the long run. Competition is enormous and the required speed is unimaginable, but still, everything is possible when you have proper awareness and a grooming education.

You would be thinking that everyone of us already knows all this mess about a race in the educational field. But can you tell me how much respect do we, as a nation, have for education? This is probably a question having a pretty dramatic answer. Truly and tragically, nearly none of us loves to study or to be educated today. We find education boring and many of us feel no shame in throwing away the hard-earned money of our parents. This is because we have many other addicting involvements which do prove to be an effective obstacle between us and education. I am never trying to restrict you from using facebook or cell phones. The actual point is something else! Hence, the real disaster occurs when the heightened energies and emotions of young age are all being wasted away and when brilliant minds happen only to learn how to increase their friend count on facebook or how to type mobile messages more quickly and effectively. This is where my focus lies! Do use them as a means of refreshing your senses but for Heaven's sake, please keep these things away from your education and studying times. You do need to learn which things are rationally worthier to be preferred over others.

These were only the reasons in our society for 'not studying'. But moreover, our reasons for 'studying' are also catastrophic over here in our society. Primarily, we are told by our elders that we have to acquire education in order to get a satisfying job and hence, a well-off life in the 'future'. We only study occasionally in order to become a doctor, an engineer or a lawyer or anything our parents or ourselves want us to become. We only study because otherwise, we have not got any other place to go except our homes. Talking about the high graders, we only study and strive for marks because we want to feel proud for being called the best student of the class. However, most of us do not bother to study even for these reasons. And hence, their goals are restricted merely to the petty desire of getting passed, whether by hook or by crook. Then, at the highest extent of morality, our fellows study only to make their parents or teachers feel proud for them. Most of you would be surely surprised because normally, these reasons are thought to be valid enough to constitute for anyone studying whole-heartedly. But my dear friends! These petty, restricted goals stand nothing in front of the real purpose of education in the eyes of a true Pakistani Muslim.

Our reasons for studying should have been different; utterly different. We have to study and we need to study with the strongest reason being the fact that Almighty Allah made education compulsory for us. The awareness of the laws of nature and finding out the mysteries of His complicated creations are in themselves, highly meritorious deeds. So we are bound to dignify education because we are Muslims.

Figure 54: Education: a necessity, an obligation

The importance of learning and education in Islam has been so justly explained in the very first revelation revealed to the Prophet of Islam (PBUH) which says:

"Read! In the name of thy Lord Who created. Created man out of a (mere) clot of congealed blood. Read! And thy Lord is most bountiful. He Who taught man the use of the pen. Taught man what he knew not." (Al-Alaq; Ayah: 1-5)

This is followed by a prayer taught in the Holy Quran:

".... And say: "O My Lord! Increase my knowledge." (Al- Taha; Ayah: 114)

Further stress upon the importance of education in Islam is put by the Holy Prophet (PBUH) who made education compulsory for every Muslim male and female, and then encouraged them to attain it no matter what difficulties stand in their way. Then to link it to practicality, the most beautiful example concerning education that we find in the Sunnah is when the prisoners of the historic Battle of Badr were freed on the condition that each of them educated ten Muslim children!

Hence, we should be studying because our religion gives a very high degree of honor to education and signifies it a lot. But being Pakistanis as well, education demands much from us. So the second reason for our studying must be to serve our nation. We should study and equip ourselves so that we can become a significant part of the people striving hard through their abilities to make Pakistan progress. Our Quaid had said:

"You must concentrate on gaining knowledge and education. It is your foremost responsibility."

We are well aware of the situation of Pakistan today and we would have to know and apply the fact that in these circumstances, knowledge is needed as a foundation to build a defensive wall against our enemies. Quaid said:

"When you have got that light of knowledge by means of education and when you have made yourselves strong economically and industrially, then you have got to prepare yourselves for defense_ a defense against external aggression and to maintain internal security." (Address to Punjab Muslim Students Federation, March 2, 1941)

Then, getting ourselves educated and acknowledged should be held by another third purpose and this purpose should be; to make us better human beings. Education is not only a bunch of facts. Rather, it is indeed a grooming phase for our minds to become more truthful, sincere, confident, brave, patriotic and humane. Therefore, we should get knowledge because Islam requires us to do so. We should get knowledge because our nation needs us and finally, we should get knowledge in order to transform us into better, civilized human beings. It is only after all these reasons that those worldly purposes otherwise common amongst us should be considered.

This was all about the importance of education in general but now let us come to our real topic which is education as the base of all progress....

Nature made education as the first rule for progress and then upheld it as a universal law. History is filled with the proofs of this status for education. Muslims were probably the first nation to recognize education as a compulsory part of life as they gained their inspiration from the Holy Quran. It was a time for Muslims when scientists like Jabir bin Hayyan and Al-Beruni were being born amongst them while on the other hand, book keeping or even book reading was considered to be a sin in Europe. This was the same time when Muslims were financially the strongest nation of the whole world and were progressing with an unstoppable speed while the Europeans were then experiencing their dark age living like wild, inhumane creatures. Then the strategy got reversed and the leadership flag of education went into European hands. Now as soon as this happened, their endless progress started. Then Europeans brought forth many scientists and researchers who based their experiments and theories on the work of Muslim pioneers and soon, a new world of information technology and new scientific developments were being nurtured by western hands. Meanwhile, Muslims were only busy in sectarian and civil wars fought only for the worldly desire of kingship. Soon, history saw a time when Mughals were busy in luxurious vices and simultaneously, the British were busy founding the universities of Oxford and Cambridge.

Figure 55: Cambridge University

Figure 56: Oxford University

Not much time had elapsed when the same British had actually wiped out the Mughals without even the slightest difficulty and were ruling the whole of India. Then in their rule here, it were the Hindus who readily accepted the new mode of education and progressed likewise while the Muslims, thinking of it as un-Islamic, were left far behind in terms of progress.

Today as well, the same rule applies everywhere. Any nation which holds education as its foremost priority is bound to progress and any nation who ignores it is bound to be doomed!

At the time of the formation of Pakistan, Quaid was fully aware of the importance of education for the new nation and had even warned us of the possible consequences of not regarding education as important. He said:

"Education is a matter of life and death for Pakistan. The world is progressing so rapidly that without requisitive advance in education, not only shall we be left behind others but may be wiped out altogether."
(Quaid on September 26, 1947 in Karachi)

But unfortunately, we failed to comply with whatever he thought or said and hence education could not find any considerable place in the priorities of any of the governments. Today also, we even fail to give

2.5% of our budget to education even when our literacy rate is hardly a half. More tragically, the yearly expense of a 'single' governmental 'palace' is greater than the annual expense of the whole education system. To add further to the agony, even our feeble educational system is being carefully divided into innumerable 'levels' for different ranks of the society. Every institution poses a unique kind of 'education' whose reliability is always directly proportional to the amount of money held as its fee. Therefore, poor children, no matter how intelligent they are, are bound to get an education which cannot play even the tiniest role in the development of the country. These children can hence, do utterly nothing except bringing only a fraction of a percent of increment in the literacy rate. Our government schools pose the worst teaching and learning conditions ever while our private schools loot the nation from every possible side. Even the medium of instruction for education is not uniform. Moreover, the syllabus taught here is only an antique set of facts with the recent teaching techniques or scientific researches given no place at all. Furthermore, our local teaching system has nothing at all to do with knowledge, because it just includes a 'copy-paste' technique comprising merely of 'rot learning'. Then the methodology is also, in most cases, very cruel for children.

Figure 57: The huge difference between two modes of schooling in the same country

Figure 58: Clearer Image of The Difference

Hence we are, for sure, far behind in education and likewise, far behind in terms of progress!

To proceed, we do need a massive as well as a positive change in the education system which is only possible with a change of our so-called 'democratic' government. We are in a grave need for a uniform education system with justice to students from every class of the society. We need educational experts and not feudal lords or governmental bureaucrats to sit on the seats designated for the area of education. Rot learning along with all the psychological and physical torture ever done to students has to be eliminated by all means. Teachers should be trained to induce a curiosity for learning and asking questions among their students rather than inducing an inborn feeling of terror in their young innocent hearts concerning their teachers. For this purpose, the level of education in government schools has to be brought up honestly and private schools have to be regularly checked on strict lines for the level of education and special prizes reserved for schools with good degree of teaching methods but all this seriously needs to be done on honest grounds. Only through this technique, a uniform teaching system and a common mode of instructions can be initiated. Teachers should be trained necessarily and uniformly all over the country to eradicate the usual worn-out teaching techniques. These steps are the only criteria on the basis of which, we can still change our possible fate and lead our nation to progress!

Our ideal education policy should be what Quaid said:

"What we have to do is to mobilize our people and build up the character of our future generation. In short, this means the highest sense of honor, integrity, selfless service to the nation and sense of responsibility, and we have to see that our people are fully equipped to play their part in the various branches of economic life in a manner which will do honor to Pakistan." (Quaid to All Pakistan Educational Conference, Karachi, November 27, 1948)

Chapter 15. Road to Success

It has been already discussed with you in full detail all over the book about the problems we face today. We have recently concluded that we, the youth of Pakistan, can save our country and give it the status in the world which it rightly deserves. Importance of education and its role in our future progress has also been told to you. Now is the time for a practical conclusion_ our future plans which can pave our way ultimately to success.

We are surely at a long distance from our target; but nevertheless, it is achievable. We have to set our goals in the skies if we want to proceed. Because Iqbal says:

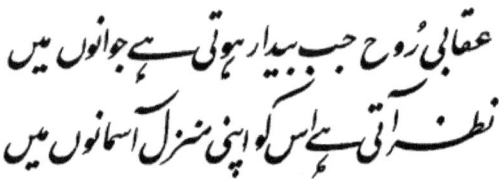

Translation:

When an eagle's spirit awakens in youthful hearts,

It sees its luminous goal beyond the starry heavens.)

However, in order to cover this long distance, our journey has to be made in gradual successive steps. These steps can then play the role of milestones along our journey on our 'road to success'.

To me, the first step that we would need to take is to dream and to set an aim_ an aim to rise up and stand in front of the conventional currents of this worn-out society, an aim to change our surroundings into the way which takes us to triumph in both worlds, an aim to save Pakistan and an aim to show the world that nothing is impossible. It clearly demands us to dream the high and the 'unachievable'. For this purpose, we would have to inculcate in ourselves, the quality of being 'idealists'. We have to dream for the impossible as the first step in making it possible. Being idealists, we have to deny the ground realities first in order to finally be able to change them. The realists have already spread enough of their hopelessness in this country and now we need idealists to uplift our Pakistan. Our Quaid was an idealist because he dreamt for the impossible but his dream, belief and diligence allowed him to achieve what once seemed unbelievably *unrealistic*. Iqbal had said about his young idealists:

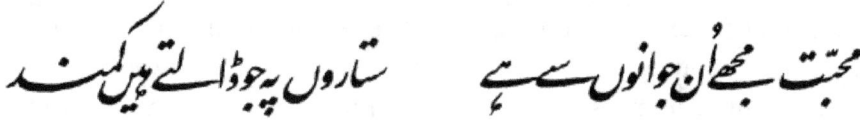

(Translation:

My love is indeed for the youth,

Who dare to throw out their ladders to the (unreachable) stars)

The second step which almost automatically follows the first one is a hope summed up with an unshaken belief in Almighty Allah's help. To work, we have to believe that whatever we are doing is worth doing and whatever we are working so hard for, can be achieved by us. I know that our resources are limited, our enemies are very cunning and the darkness around us is very thick. But no matter what it is, I know that my country has to rise because I believe that whatever I may do for it is right and Allah always helps the one who strives for the righteous cause. We should know that:

نہیں ہے ناامید اقبال اپنی کشتِ ویراں سے   ذرا نم ہو تو یہ مٹی بہت زرخیز ہے ساقی

(Translation:

But of his barren acres Iqbal will not despair,

A little rain and harvests shall wave at last, O Saki!)

After this hope and belief, the next requirement is a dauntless ambition, will and determination. To stick to one's cause despite all difficulties is the secret to success. Therefore, consistency to purpose is needed desperately. Along with all these feelings another feeling of bravery and courage is also essential. We have to become fearless of negative consequences because our purpose is solely rebellious to the existing system. Resistance would be there, obstacles and difficulties would also be there; but we have to acknowledge the fact that once we overcome our own inner fear, nothing remains difficult.

"Do not be afraid of the briskness of the opponent wind, O Eagle!

The reason why it blows is nothing but to heighten your flight"

The third step after dream, hope and belief is to produce in ourselves, the feeling of utmost pride for our identity. Succeeding in convincing ourselves to feel proud to be a Pakistani and a Muslim in all circumstances is in itself a considerable achievement. Our identity deserves to be felt proud of and we have to do it while bringing a true change in our country. In reality, being a Pakistani, it should be our foremost aim to firstly feel proud of our own identity ourselves and then strive with all our might and main to make us strong enough to stand up, look into eyes of the whole world and then claim and own that we are Pakistani Muslims and are surely proud to be so. I have already told enough reasons constituting for us feeling proud of being a Muslim and a Pakistani well in detail in one of the previous chapters. So I do hope that you would surely feel proud for your identity at least from now onwards because we have to do it if we want to succeed. Remember! Feeling proud for our identity demands us to become a

'Shaheen' of Iqbal in order to fly like a crowned king among the vastness of the skies.

تو شاہیں ہے پرواز ہے کام تیرا   تیرے سامنے آسماں اور بھی ہیں

(Translation:

You are an eagle, flight is your vocation.

You have other skies stretching out before you.)

The next step is, obviously, to change ourselves practically. This is, without any doubt, the most important and the most difficult task to be accomplished. Going through a complete turmoil to change one's whole being is never an easy task but we have to do it in order to change to system. We are the new generation and are surely better than the recent previous ones in many aspects. But we have to change ourselves even more to fit rightly into the criteria needed for a positive change in our society and in our country.

This change in us also comes in parts with the first the most important part being the one to change ourselves into better Muslims. Our Beloved Prophet (PBUH) had said:

"The greatest Jihad is to fight against the evil passions of oneself."

This Jihad is the whole secret behind us succeeding in changing ourselves to better Muslims. We would have to be better in behavior with everyone and shun the horrible third class street culture of abuses. Muslims have always held a dignity over other nations and this dignity is, always hidden in their behavior. However, we are also in a dire need of reading the translation of Holy Quran at least once. I can bet that we can find answers to all our queries and questions whether directly or indirectly in it. We have to fortify our belief in accountability as well. To do it; just think once before doing anything wrong that there is someone up there, looking at us and to Him we shall be held answerable.

Figure 59: Salat_ the sole distinguisher for being a Muslim

Praying five times a day forms the basis of Islam and anyone who fails to do even this, should reconsider his claim of being a Muslim because the Holy Quran says:

"..... And this (Salat) is surely difficult except for those who are fearful."
(Al-Baqarah; Ayah: 45)

These were some basic and most difficult changes which we have to make in ourselves. I do know that perfection is simply impossible for people full of flaws like us. I cannot even assure you of myself fulfilling all requirements of this change except a promise of trying my best. But Allah is verily the All-Forgiving, Most Merciful. So we should at least try to our fullest and then leave the results to Allah. This change would surely make your life as easy and comfortable as sleeping on a bed of roses. Because:

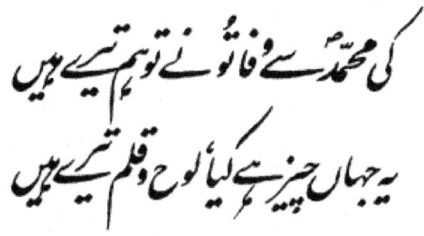

(Translation:

To my Muhammad (SAWW) be but true and have conquered Me;

The world is nothing; you will command My Pen of Destiny.)

The second change that we have to make in ourselves is becoming a better Pakistani. We are, obviously, the citizens of this state and being so, we become bound to abide by the rules of the state no matter how weak the real enforcement is. We have to change ourselves and we have to follow all rules in every aspect and this becomes mandatory to us when we call ourselves Pakistanis. We also have to change the elderly heirloom of corruption which is creeping everywhere in our society. As we are changing ourselves so we would have to be firm in our honesty and sincerity to the state. We would have to love Pakistan even more and hence, prefer its interests over our interests to become a good Pakistani. Moreover, we have to respect Pakistan ourselves and then make others respect it as well. We also have to work hard all our life only for our country because this land has an innumerable amount of debt over us and we have to repay it.

The third change in us that automatically comes along with the previous ones is becoming a better human being. So we all promise here that we would surely try our best never to lie, cheat, abuse nor to do even the slightest harm to the honor and dignity of our beloved country.

After changing ourselves, the next step is to bring a clear change in our surroundings and our system. Although the system around us is so horribly strangled into every vice that changing it seems to be impossible. But remember, we have just learnt that we are idealists now so we are now to dream of the impossible in order to make it possible. Practically, the tool which can be instantly used to bring a considerable change is our vote. Vote is an authority and every authority, no matter how small it is, is always a sacred award by Almighty for which we would surely be held answerable. Therefore, while voting we would have to consider everything and would use the vital power of vote to change the system and bring in new, honest and truthful leaders instead of following the same tradition of giving generations of feudal to get turns in the Assembly again and again.

The next thing which can be done at the moment is the raising of our voice of denial against this system. The power of the people is surely greater than the people in power and this is the right time to use this power. We are strongly fed up by this system but we can never change it unless we raise a protesting voice against it. But please! We have to bring a positive change in our heinous methods of protesting as well. If we burn shops or vehicles or if we destroy the traffic lights, poles or other civil service equipment; it seriously does no harm to those who are living in luxurious palaces and signing our death warrants. If we want to protest, we should do it peacefully in a civilized manner and a method which is more suited to educated 'human beings'. However, it is not necessary that mere protesting is the only way to announce our disagreement concerning the system. At a much lower level, we can attain it simply by speaking and by trying to stop any 'conventional' bad deed happening in front of our eyes. Holy Prophet (PBUH) said:

"Whoever of you sees an evil action let him change it with its hand, and if he is not able to do so then with his tongue, and if he is not able to do so then with his heart, and that is the weakest of the faith."

We can surely change the system if we declare war against it in every aspect. For example, if we want good marks when why don't we just study instead of relying on the evil replacement, that is, cheating. We have to stop it now; for enough has already been destroyed.

Another huge step towards the betterment of the country and the change of the system is the eradication of feudal control over the country. All these political parties assuming power turn by turn are headed by the worst feudal lords known to history and all of their election candidates are also feudal lords of lower ranks. These people actually rule over their small territory of villages like kings and they just keep local people as slaves buying each and every vote. These feudal lords are the real problem for the country as they become the base for all other problems faced by our country. These feudal lords then control the government and hence, the people of Pakistan as well. However, more tragic is the 'Thana' culture with all law-enforcement forces also behaving as the meager subordinates of the same feudal lords. These feudal lords are the people who live a life of utmost luxury when a considerable majority of the masses is forced to live a life below the poverty line dragging on their lives in unbearable conditions. These people are the real criminals of the society and also of this country and hence, we have to fight against these criminals as well in order to succeed as a nation. Laws and restrictions on government level are essential to be passed against feudalism just to break the continuity of this corrupt system. However, as we are discussing things on our level so what we can do against feudalism is just to condemn it to the extent we can and spread awareness in local country people that they can defeat these feudal lords if they all stand up in a united way against them. For verily, it is only their lack of awareness and lack of acknowledgement of their abilities which makes them and their generations lifelong slaves of these brutal feudal lords who think they even own the lives of the poor people of their villages.

Another extremely important requirement for our success is our unity for our purpose. We would have to destroy all walls of sectarian division and walk together by joining hands to a fully common purpose of our national success. However, it is so true that when we all would be busy working for Pakistan there would be simply no time with anyone to fight with others on such petty issues. Anyhow, we do have to stop thinking as Punjabis, Sindhis, Baluchis, Pathans, Muhajirs or Kashmiris and rather, we should start thinking only as Pakistanis now. We are surely in dire need of unity and I do assure you that when you would start thinking nothing else except being a Pakistani, you would surely find out that all these provincial identities belong to you. So we should think that every Pakistani is a Punjabi, Sindhi, Baluchi, Pathan, Muhajir and Kashmiri and after that, we would automatically feel proud for all these identities because these all are Pakistan and Pakistan is never complete if even one of them is missing. We have already had a very bitter experience with our province of Bengal in 1971. Our corrupt leadership convinced them that they were nothing except slaves to West Pakistan because they were never given their justified share in Pakistan's resources. Although, at a common level, our forefathers regarded them as brothers but our traitor leaders had done their job. We must be warned that they are trying to do the same once again but this time, with Baluchistan. This is a very critical stage for testing our unity. So please, shun divisions at least now and become practical brothers to save the integrity of Pakistan.

Our great Quaid-e-Azam Muhammad Ali Jinnah had said about our unity:

"If you will work in cooperation, forgetting the past, burying the hatchet, you are bound to succeed. If you change your past and work together in a spirit that everyone of you, no matter to what community he belongs, no matter what relations he had with you in the past, no matter what is his caste, color or creed, is first, second and last a citizen of this state with equal rights, privileges and obligations, there will be no end to the progress you will make..... even as regards Muslims you have Pathans, Punjabis, Shias, Sunnis and so on..." (Quaid's address to constituent Assembly, August 1947)

Being the youth of Pakistan, we would be soon going into different professions and would surely become the backbone of the country. Therefore, another step is a continuous toil towards our success. We have to work extremely hard for this change as Iqbal said:

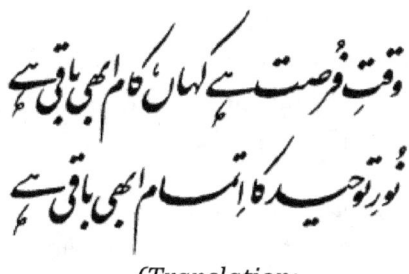

(Translation:

There is no time for idle rest, much yet remains undone.

The light of the 'Tawhid' still awaits its completion.)

But we would have to work so hard never for ourselves, but for our country. Our Quaid said:

"I insist you to strive. Work, work and only work for satisfaction with patience, humbleness and serve the nation." (All India Muslim Students Conference Jalandhar, 15th November,1942)

For this purpose, all our abilities and talents must be utilized to their fullest only for our country. We have to make ourselves accustomed to difficult conditions in order to work hard for our success. Luxury should have nothing to do with us.

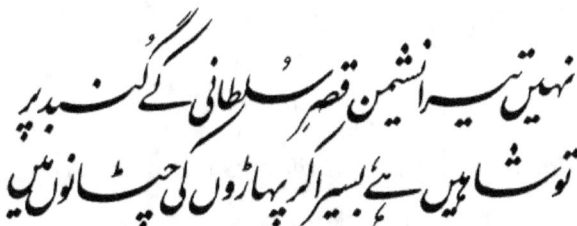

(Translation:

Thy abode is not on the dome of a royal palace,

You are an eagle and should live in the rocks of the mountains.)

Moreover, we should know that the path we are aiming demands heavy sacrifices all over the long journey and for this we have to prepare ourselves mentally, physically and psychologically for all responsibilities. Our Quaid said:

"Development is being sought in every walk of life and you have to take on this process of development. Are you preparing to take on tomorrow's responsibilities? Are you building your capacity? Are you trained enough? If no, then go and prepare yourself because this is the time to prepare yourself for future responsibilities." (Guidance for students through Ministry of Education)

Another important step towards our success is the recognition of our real enemies and our ultimate success over them. You have been already told in detail about all the enemies we face and most of the hidden intrigues should also be open to you now. Now it is time to work and to make the enemies acknowledge the fact once again that Muslims can never be defeated.

کوئی اندازہ کرسکتا ہے اُس کے زورِ بازو کا

نگاہِ مردِ مومن سے بدل جاتی ہیں تقدیریں

(Translation:

Can anyone guess at the strength of his arm?

By the glance of the man who is a true believer, even destiny is changed.)

Iqbal also said about the bravery of us Muslims:

ماسوی اللہ کے لیے آگ ہے تکبیر تری   تو مسلماں ہو تو تقدیر ہے تدبیر تری

(Translation:

For all else but God, your Takbeer is the ferocious fire;

If you a Muslim truly are, your effort is your fate.)

Let me remind you one thing here. Our enemies are not at all brave. They are merely cunning and their cunningness can be easily defeated by our love for Islam and Pakistan because these are the only things which they always try to target and remove the pathway in order to defeat our enemies has been told by Quaid:

"Get out of tranquility and step into practical life. Dedicate your facilities to seek improvement in every field to make the condition of people better. It is only then we can be strong enough to counter threats to our nation and to defeat our enemies." (Message to Bohar Students of Karachi, January 13, 1941)

So, we are to work till our last breath with unity, faith and discipline to help us proceed and succeed in our goals and ambitions. However, what is our role in the country's success all starts from the all important education and hence, we just have to study well today to tackle with the problems of the country tomorrow. Although the 'change ourselves' procedure should start today, but before you give this change a full political outlook, you would have to complete your education first.

Therefore, although our goal is high but our ambitions are also high and we are surely ready to bring a change. Our land and our people have had enough of their bad days and now it is our responsibility to return them their good days. Our enthusiasm and our practicality is what our nation needs the most and we have to never let it be disappointed from us. However, just remember one thing! The good days are not too far. Iqbal said:

کتابِ ملّتِ بیضا کی پھر شیرازہ بندی ہے
یہ شاخِ ہاشمی کرنے کو ہے پھر برگ و بر پیدا

(Translation:

This book of Radiant Community is receiving a new binding,

The Hashimite branch is once more ready to bring forth new leaves and fruit.)

So, get up my friends! And grab your goal. For the nation seriously needs you all.

Special Thanks to the following Sources:

1. ”Islam; Beliefs and Practices” by Yasmin Malik

2. ”Islamiat” by Farkhanda Noor Muhammad

3. ”The Environment of Pakistan” by Huma Naz Sethi

4. ”Pakistan; History, Culture and Government” by Nigel Smith

5. ”The History and Culture of Pakistan” by Nigel Kelly

6. http://en.wikipedia.org/japan/ (for information about present day Japan)

7. http://www.clearquran.com/ (for English translation of the Holy Quran)

8. http://www.worldwar2history.info/ (for details about the World War II)

9. http://m-a-jinnah.blogspot.com/ (for quotes of Quaid-e-Azam)

10. http://www.brecorder.com/muhammad-ali-jinnah/ (for quotes of Quaid-e-Azam)

11. http://iqbalurdu.blogspot.com/ (for English translation of Iqbal poetry)